Using this book

Each technique is illustrated with a sequence of photographs, or diagrams where they are easier to understand. There are arrows between the photographs to show in which direction to follow the sequence.

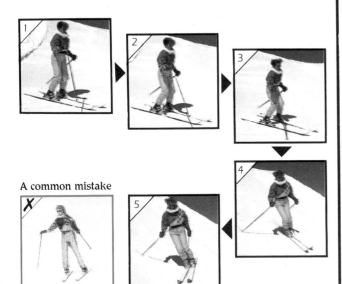

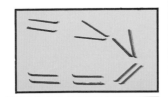

Common mistakes

Common mistakes made in a particular technique are illustrated to help you recognize when you make them yourself. In the sequence above, for example, both knees should be bent to complete a turn successfully.

These tips are highlighted in a pink box with a cross in the top left-hand corner.

Ski positions

Alongside some photo sequences are bird's-eye view diagrams of the correct ski positions for each step.

Leg positions

In most techniques it is important that most of your weight is balanced over your lower ski. The pictures are shaded to show you on which leg to balance.

Shading

Warning!

Do not attempt any techniques highlighted in a red box without expert help from a ski instructor, as they can be dangerous. Safety rules are also highlighted in this way. Read the information in these boxes very carefully.

Skiing words

Some of the words used in this book are to do with the slope of the mountain and the direction in which you are skiing or turning. These are explained below. There is also a glossary on pages 61-62 which explains other unfamiliar words.

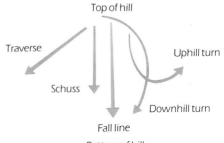

Fall line: the most direct line down a slope.
Traversing: skiing across the fall line.
Schussing: skiing straight down the fall line.
Turning uphill: a turn made up into the slope.
Turning downhill: a turn made across the fall line.

Edging: you edge your skis by pressing against either their inside or outside, upper or lower sides. The sides of your skis have steel edges which bite into the snow. In this diagram, the skier is standing at right angles to the fall line with the upper sides of the skis "edged" into the slope to stop him sliding downhill.

Skis edged - upper edges biting into the snow.

Fall line

In this book, the terms inside, outside, upper and lower are often used instead of left and right where it is clearer. Inside and outside skis, hips and poles depend on the direction in which you are turning, as illustrated below.

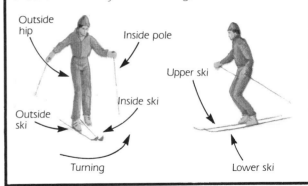

Outside hip

Inside pole

Outside ski

Inside ski

Turning

Upper ski

Lower ski

Getting started

The following 16 pages give an outline of the techniques you need to learn to become a competent skier. You may find that the names used for some techniques, and the way they are taught, varies from country to country. The basic techniques, though, are fairly standard.

Use this section as a guide only. The best way to learn and improve is with ski school instruction and lots of practice on the slopes.

Skiing clothes

Skiing clothes should keep you warm and dry as well as allowing you to move freely. Your body can become very warm whilst skiing and then cool rapidly when you sit on a chairlift. It is best to wear at least three layers of clothes: first, a layer made of natural fibres to carry moisture away from the skin; second a layer to absorb the moisture, and third an outer wind proof layer which also allows your body to "breathe".

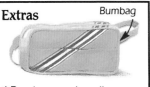

Extras
Bumbag

* Bumbags and small rucksacks are useful for carrying extra clothing and sun cream.

* Jackets with detachable sleeves are useful for warmer spring skiing.

* Use long thermal underwear or tights under trousers in cold weather.

This picture shows you how to protect the different parts of your body.

Head

About 20% of your body heat is lost through your head, so wear a hat, or carry one with you in case it gets cold. Keep ears warm with a head band, ear muff or scarf.

You may need a balaclava or long scarf to wrap around your whole face on very cold chair lifts*.

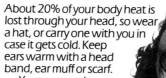

Hands and wrists

Use leather gloves or mittens. Gloves will give you better grip, but mittens are warmer. Use silk inner gloves for extra warmth in very cold weather.

Gloves and mittens should have a long, close-fitting cuff to cover your wrists.

Carrying your skis

The safest way to carry your skis is to balance them on their sides on your shoulder, ski tips in front, as shown above. Be careful when you turn around not to hit someone.

Hold your skis together by locking the "ski stoppers" or tie them together with their "safety straps", if fitted (see page 27). You can also buy rubber ties from a ski shop.

Eyes and skin

The higher you go up a mountain, the stronger the sun's ultra violet rays will be. You need to protect yourself from this, and glare from the snow.

Use polarized sun glasses or goggles to protect your eyes from "snow-blindness". Use yellow lenses when light is poor - when it is snowing for instance. Use high protection factor sun cream for all exposed skin and protective cream for your lips.

Waist

It is important to keep the trunk of your body warm for it to function properly. Make sure you have no gaps around your waist where snow and cold air can enter.

Lower legs

Nylon gaiters keep the bottom of ski trousers dry and snow out of your boots.

Feet

You should wear only one pair of socks in ski boots but if you get very cold feet, use silk inner socks.

*See page 20.

USBORNE BOOK OF
SKIING

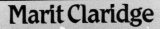

Marit Claridge
Designed by Nerissa Davies
Edited by Tony Potter

Illustrated by:
Mick Posen, Chris Lyon and Guy Smith

Special location photography by Mark Junak

Alpine — Les Diablerets, Switzerland
Freestyle — Tignes, France
Cross-country — Zwiesel, West Germany

Ski demonstrators:
Eric Mermod, Micheline Morerod, Jean-François Morerod, Julia Snell,
Mike Whealey, Leonie Coppard, Nigel Winter and Ben Rix

Consultant editors:
Mike Nemesvary, Nick Fickling, David Goldsmith and John Shedden
With thanks to Moira Butterfield, Iain Ashman and Pam Corfield

Contents

About this book

This book is both for beginners and more advanced skiers. It explains with step-by-step photographs and diagrams how to do the basic techniques of downhill (or alpine) and cross-country (or nordic) skiing.

The organization, judging and scoring of the major competition skiing events shown on T.V. - from slalom to ballet - are explained in detail. You can also find out how to do simple ballet steps yourself.

If you are planning a skiing trip, there are tips on choosing a resort, things to look out for on prepared ski runs (called "pistes") and lots of information on weather and safety. To get in trim, there are special skiing exercises to do at home on pages 56-59.

You can also find out why skis are shaped the way they are and how they help you turn, and about the history of skiing.

First published in 1986 by Usborne Publishing Ltd, 20 Garrick Street, London WC2E 9BJ, England.

Putting on skis

When putting on your skis for the first time, find a flat area of snow and lay them down parallel. Check that the bindings, which clamp your boots to your skis*, are in the open position. The "ski stoppers" will stop the skis from sliding until you step into the binding.

Clear snow from the sole of one boot with sharp taps with your pole, or use the pole tip to scrape it away.

Put your toe into the front of the binding and make sure that your boot is centred over it.

Press your heel down until the binding clicks into position. Do the same with your other boot.

Correct posture

It is important to have a good posture on skis, as shown on the right, from the minute you start skiing. Skiing in the correct posture is safe, efficient and comfortable.

You can practise your posture whilst standing on the flat.

Arms slightly forward and relaxed, elbows bent.

Ankles and knees bent and legs slightly apart.

The angle of your boots * will help you to bend your ankles more than usual.

Feet slightly apart, weight balanced equally over both.

Head up.

Upper body in relaxed, standing posture.

Things to avoid

Head too low.

Upper body bent too far forward.

Arms stiff and too far forward.

Hips and bottom sticking out.

Knees not bending.

Holding poles

Loop the pole straps around your wrists so that you do not lose the pole if you fall and let go.

1

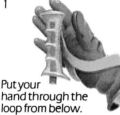

Put your hand through the loop from below.

2

Grip the handle firmly over the strap.

Getting used to your skis

Try these simple exercises to get used to wearing skis.

Lean your body forwards and backwards to feel the support of your boots.

Slide each ski backwards and forwards without lifting up your feet.

Lift each ski in turn and twist it from left to right to improve your balance.

Twist your knees from side to side and feel how your edges dig into the snow.

* See pages 26-27 for more on bindings and boots.

Walking, climbing, turning and falling

Walking on skis

To walk on alpine skis, slide alternate skis forward. Keep your skis parallel and slightly apart, take short strides and do not try to lift your heels - a bit like shuffling your feet. You can use your poles for support and to push with.

Slide your right ski forward, together with your left pole.

Push off on your left pole while sliding the left ski forwards.

Swing your right pole forwards in time with moving your left ski.

Walking uphill

As a beginner, you need to be able to walk up a slope to practise a few downhill runs. When you become more experienced there will still be times when you need to be able to walk uphill.

Unlike cross-country skis (see pages 28-33), alpine skis have no grip, so you can not walk directly up a slope. There are two methods of walking uphill, "side-stepping" and the "herringbone".

Follow the photo sequences on the right by starting at the bottom and reading up the page.

Side-stepping

The side-step is the least tiring way of climbing up a steep slope. Start by standing with your skis at right angles to the fall line and then step your skis, one at a time, sideways up the hill.

Keep your upper ski forwards and your hips bent into the hill to edge your skis. Lift your upper ski and put it down on its upper edge. Lift up the lower ski. Use your poles for support and balance.

Step up lower ski.

Lift upper ski.

Skis edged.

Step up lower ski.

Lift upper ski.

Start here

The herringbone

The herringbone is more tiring than side-stepping but it is faster on gentle slopes and short ascents. Begin by facing up the hill with your skis in a wide "V".

Herringbone position

Face uphill with your skis in wide "V". Push your knees into the slope to dig in the inside edges. Hold your poles behind the skis for support with your palm over the handle, thumb and fingers downwards, as shown below.

Pole grip

Grip here.

Step up

Grip here.

Step up ski.

Lean on poles.

Grip here.

Step up ski.

Start here

Make sure that your right ski is gripping the snow and step up the left ski. Then, step the right ski up, just above the left ski. Carry on, stepping up each leg in turn.

Turning on the flat

The simplest way to change direction on level ground is the "clock turn", which is named after the pattern it makes in the snow. From the standing position, step your skis around one by one in a circle. You can keep either the ski tips or the ski tails at the centre of the circle.

1 Start with your skis parallel and your poles planted either side of you.

2 Lift the tip of your left ski, swing it sideways and put it down about 30cm away.

Pivot around the tails of your skis.

Step onto this ski.

Use poles for balance.

3 Lift the tip of the right ski and swing it round next to the left ski.

4 Continue taking small steps until you are facing the direction you want.

Falling correctly

Knowing how to fall correctly is important in skiing, particularly as a beginner. When you are learning to ski, falling can also be a useful way of stopping. Whatever the reason for falling, a controlled fall is unlikely to result in injury.

If a fall is unavoidable, keep calm. Just before you reach the snow straighten your legs.

Keep your hands up and in front of your body.

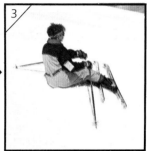
Keep your skis below your body and try to end up with the skis at right angles to the fall line.

Getting up

Having fallen, you need to be in the correct position, as in step 3 above, to stand up. Your skis should be parallel, at right angles to the fall line and downhill of your body. Use your poles to push yourself up as shown to the right.

Draw your skis up to your body and plant your poles uphill and close to your sides.

Edge your skis, and push yourself up on your poles to stand upright.

Putting on skis on a slope

If your skis come off when you fall on a slope you need to be able to put them on without sliding downhill.

Place your skis across the hill at right angles to the fall line. Put your lower ski on first.

Edge your lower ski and then put on your upper ski. Use your poles for balance and support.

Bad falls

Most skiing injuries happen when people try to stop an unavoidable fall. Try not to be afraid of falling. Remember that the safest way to fall is to sit sideways into the slope and to straighten your legs. Ski bindings are designed to release in a bad fall, which helps to lessen the chance of your hurting yourself (see page 27 for more on ski bindings).

Schussing and snowploughing

The first run

The basic aim of skiing is to flow freely down a mountain. The simplest alpine manoeuvre is to ski straight down the fall line, called "schussing". The nursery slopes will allow you to come to a gradual halt so you do not need to worry about stopping.

The instructions on these pages show you how to schuss* and snowplough.

Turning into the fall line

Turn your skis to face down the fall line, ready for your first run, as shown here. Use your poles for support while stepping your skis round one by one.

Start with your skis across the slope and your weight on the lower ski. Keep your skis edged all the time.

Plant your poles down the slope and lean on them while you step the uphill ski around slightly.

Schussing

Start with your skis parallel, hip width apart, and balance equally over both skis. Relax your body, with your ankles, knees and hips bent slightly. Hold your poles out from your sides, as shown to the right.

Ski straight down the slope until you stop.

Common mistake

If you do not bend your knees, ankles and hips when schussing, your skis will accelerate from under you. You may lose control and fall backwards as shown in the two pictures on the right.

The knees, ankles and hips are not bent forwards.

Schussing exercise

Practise climbing up gentle slopes and skiing straight down again until you feel confident. Then try bending and stretching on the run as shown to the right. This will help your balance. Keep your skis hip width apart.

Start schussing with your arms held out to the side.

Bend right down and try to touch your toes.

Stand up again as you continue to ski downhill.

Bumps and dips

Most slopes, even gentle nursery slopes, are not completely smooth, so you will need to be able to ski over bumps and dips without being thrown off balance. Bend your knees as your feet ride over the bump and then straighten your legs as you come over the other side. In this way your legs will absorb the shock of the bump.

Keep forwards for better balance.

Bend your legs.

Stretch your legs.

Straighten your body.

*More advanced schussing is discussed on page 19.

3

Step the lower ski next to the upper ski. Continue taking small steps until you are facing downhill.

X

Skier loses control and falls as his skis accelerate.

4

Stretch up high, standing on the balls of your feet.

Legs absorb shock.

The snowplough

Before you take lifts* up to steeper, more varied slopes, you need to learn how to control your speed and stop. The snowplough can be used for gliding, braking and stopping, as well as for turning, which is explained on page 10.

The correct snowplough position is shown below. Once you are familiar with it, try skiing down a gentle slope and coming to a halt, as shown in the photographs on the right.

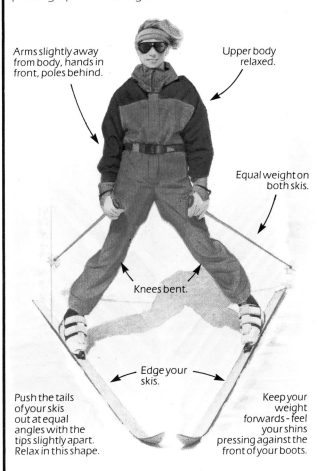

Arms slightly away from body, hands in front, poles behind.

Upper body relaxed.

Equal weight on both skis.

Knees bent.

Edge your skis.

Push the tails of your skis out at equal angles with the tips slightly apart. Relax in this shape.

Keep your weight forwards - feel your shins pressing against the front of your boots.

Snowplough position

Practise standing in the snowplough position on level ground, as shown above. Your skis form a "V" shape, with the tips together and tails apart - opposite to the herringbone position where the "V" is formed with the ski tails together. Your weight should be on the inside edges of your skis.

Common mistake

X

Legs stiff.

Bend at your ankles and knees, not stiffly from the waist as shown here or you will have no control.

Snowplough and snowplough stop

1

Begin with your skis facing straight down the fall line.

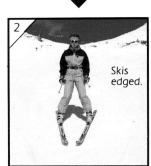

2

Skis edged.

Sink and then push your ski tails out into the snowplough position.

3

Push against heels.

To brake, open your skis into a wider "V" by sinking down further.

4

Press hard against your skis with both feet and you will come to a halt. Push equally on both skis.

* See pages 20-21 for how to use lifts.   9

Snowplough exercise and turns, and traversing

Snowplough exercise

Start skiing down the slope in the schuss position and then push your skis into a snowplough. Try going in and out of the snowplough by opening and closing your skis. Keep practising until you feel confident that you can slow down and stop when and where you want to.

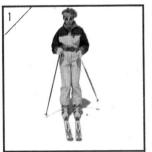

1. Start in a schuss position, with your skis parallel and flat on the snow.

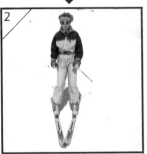

2. Sink down, pushing your skis into a slight "V". Edge your skis.

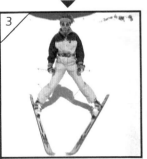

3. Widen the angle of the "V" and push against your heels to brake.

4. Rise up again and glide your skis parallel and flat on the snow.

Repeat movements 1-4. Notice how your speed increases and decreases.

Snowplough turns

Another way of controlling speed is to turn across the fall line. Snowplough turns are the simplest to learn. In a snowplough, glide down the fall line with your weight balanced equally over both skis. Move your head over your left ski to turn right and over your right ski to turn left. The photograph sequence here shows a turn to the right.

Practise turns to the right and left across the fall line. Keep your hips central between your skis and let your knees and feet do the turning. Do not try and steer with your whole body.

When the turn is complete, relax the pressure on your left ski and press equally against both skis. Your skis will turn back towards the fall line.

5.

Correct turning positions

Do not try to steer the turn with your hips and shoulders. Your feet and knees should do all the work. Move your head over the steering ski and try to keep looking down the hill. The pictures on the right show the correct positions for turns to the right and left.

1. Start by skiing in a plough down the fall line, with your weight balanced equally.

2. Sink down slightly, and push gently against the left ski.

3. Keep your head over the left ski. Your hips should be in the middle of the plough.

4. Keep pressing against your left ski and keep it edged. Your right ski should be fairly flat on the snow.

Bend knees.

Head over right ski.

Head over left ski.

Turning left   Turning right

Linked turns

To link up a series of turns across the fall line, the end of each turn becomes the beginning of the next.

Push against your left ski to turn right.

Push against your right ski to turn left.

Rise slightly.

Rise slightly.

Bend knees.

Keep your head over the steering ski.

Push against ski.

Traversing

Once you can link up a series of turns, you will be able to control and steer your outer ski quite well. Try skiing across the slope with your upper ski parallel to the lower ski. This is called traversing and is faster than the snowplough, as your skis are not constantly braking.

Keep your arms in front of your body, with your poles behind.

Bend your knees.

Both your skis should be on their inside edges, with most of your weight on the lower ski.

Traverse position

Keep your head over the lower ski. This transfers your weight onto the lower ski so that you can grip with it. Bend your knees and keep your upper ski slightly forwards, as shown below.

Balance test

When traversing, you will sometimes slip sideways slightly. It is important to keep your head over the lower ski to keep your balance. Try the test below, to prove to yourself that this is a stable position.

Stand with your skis parallel to the fall line. Ask a friend to take your lower pole and try to pull you down the slope. You will find that your head goes over your lower ski, and it is almost impossible for your friend to pull you over.

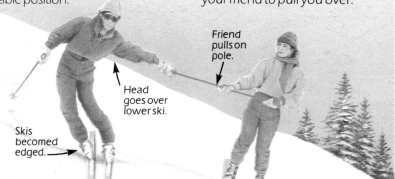

Head goes over lower ski.

Skis becomed edged.

Friend pulls on pole.

Traversing exercises and side-slipping

Skiing in a traverse

Traversing is slower than schussing straight down the fall line, but your speed depends on the line you take down the slope. Practise traversing at different angles down the slope. Concentrate on keeping your body in a good traversing posture, as shown in the exercises below.

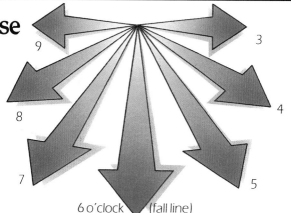

Traverse lines down a slope

The possible lines down a slope are like the hands of a clock, with 6 o'clock being the fall line and 3 and 9 o'clock at right angles to the fall line.

Traversing exercises

With modern skis and boots, traversing is very easy. You will find that the three exercises to the right will help you improve your ability to traverse, particularly on steep slopes or in variable snow conditions.

Try each exercise several times and in exercise 3, try also lifting your lower ski, as this will improve your balance.

Hold your poles together, as shown, and align them with your shoulders, hips, knees and ski tips.

This makes all the axes of your body parallel, giving you a good traversing posture.

Traverse at a gentle angle (about 4 o'clock), bend over outwards and try to touch your lower ankle.

This presses your hips into the slope and makes you lean over the lower ski. It also edges the skis.

During a traverse, lift your upper ski off the snow and hold it up for a second or two.

This keeps your weight on the lower ski and also helps you lean over the lower ski.

Slowing down

If you are going too fast on a traverse, use the snowplough to slow down. Bend down slightly and push the tail of the lower ski out into a snowplough. This is called stemming and is also used in turns*.

Sink down

Start by traversing across the slope.

Edge your skis.

Stem out your lower ski and push against it.

The stemed lower ski will act as a brake.

Stepping uphill to stop

A simple way of stopping from a traverse, is to step your skis uphill. Lift your upper ski and place it at a shallow angle uphill, and then lift your lower ski parallel. Step up again if necessary.

Plant your upper pole as you lift the upper ski.

Place the upper ski down, angled uphill.

Lift the lower ski up parallel to the upper ski.

*See page 15 for stem christie turns.

Side-slipping

Side-slipping is a very useful technique for slipping down a steep slope in complete control where turns are difficult.

Start in a stationary traverse position. Push your knees away from the hill, with your head over the lower ski, to release your edges and start slipping.

Stand across the fall line with your skis parallel and edged.

Head over lower ski.

Push both knees downhill to flatten your skis and begin to side-slip.

While slipping, put more weight on lower ski. Use your edges to slow down.

Move your thighs sideways into the hill to tilt onto the upper edges and stop.

Side-slip from a traverse

If you find it difficult to begin side-slipping from stationary, you can side-slip from a traverse, as shown below. You start the slide by pushing out your lower ski, keeping your head over it. Keep edging gently to control the speed of your side-slip.

Close-up of skis

Skis edged.

Skis side-slipping.

Keep your head over the lower ski.

Edge gently to control your speed.

Move your head over your lower ski. Your upper ski will flatten on the snow and follow the lower ski. Push off from the upper ski if necessary.

Push out your lower ski so it begins to skid.

Start in a traverse.

Side-slip forwards and backwards

You can side-slip forwards and backwards down a slope by tilting forwards and backwards, as shown to the right.

Forwards side-slip.

Begin side-slipping and tilt forwards so that your weight is on the front of your skis.

Backwards side-slip.

Tilt back so that you can feel your weight on your heels.

Your skis will swing so that the tips point up and the tails down.

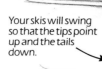

Practise tilting back and forth ▶ until you can control the direction of the slip.

13

Practice exercise and stem christie

Practice exercise

The techniques introduced so far enable you to descend most easy slopes. This will usually involve using more than one technique. Try the exercise shown here, which links up the techniques covered already, whilst skiing down a gentle to moderate slope.

START HERE

Snowplough

Tight snowplough turns.

Bigger snowplough turns.

Traverse

Side-slip

Turn

Traverse

Side-slip

Traverse

Turn

Step uphill to stop.

Once you have mastered these techniques and are able to adapt them to most slopes, you can begin to learn to ski with your skis parallel. The next five pages introduce further techniques which will help you to ski faster and more fluently down steeper slopes and move towards parallel turns. As you progress, invent exercises for yourself to link up each technique you learn.

Planting your poles

The stem christie turn, described on the right, and parallel turns involve planting your inside pole. This helps you keep your balance and gives support as you transfer your weight from one ski to the other. The timing and positioning of the pole plant has to be just right, as shown below.

Sink down and firmly plant the inside pole to the side of your lower ski, between the boot and ski tip.

Straighten your legs as you push off from the pole and transfer your weight onto the outside ski.

Keep your hands low and slightly in front of you and pull the pole out as you ski past it.

Hopping pole exercise

If you find it difficult to get used to planting your poles on turns, try this exercise. On a schuss, bend down and plant one pole and then hop up, straightening your legs. Continue bending and hopping up on your skis using alternate poles.

1 Starting in a schuss, plant your right pole beside your right ski, between the tip of your ski and your boot.

2 Spring up straight and hop up the tails of your skis. Bring the left pole forward, ready to plant.

3 Sink down forwards by bending your knees until the pole is next to your boot.

Stem christie

Stem christies are faster turns than snowploughs and can be done with either an uphill or downhill stem.

Begin this turn by stemming out the upper ski into a half snowplough as shown to the right.

1 Start by skiing across the fall line, with your weight on the lower ski. Bring your lower pole forwards.

2 Stem out your upper ski – this tilts it against its inside edge and helps you turn towards the fall line.

3 Sink down as you plant your lower pole beside the lower ski, between the tip and your boot.

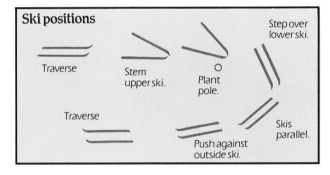

Ski positions

Traverse

Stem upper ski.

Plant pole.

Step over lower ski.

Traverse

Push against outside ski.

Skis parallel.

4 Step against the outside ski and lift your unweighted inside ski parallel to it.

5 Sink down and push your knees forwards and edge your skis. Keep facing downhill.

6 Steer the turn by continuous pressure against the outside ski and by turning your legs slightly.

7 When the turn is complete, straighten into the normal traverse position ready for the next turn.

A common mistake

If your lower leg is straight as ▶ you try to steer into the turn, as shown on the right, you will not be able to edge and control your skis. Both knees should be bent.

Parallel turns

Parallel uphill turn

The parallel uphill turn is a technique for turning away from the fall line with your skis parallel. Use it for braking and stopping as well as for developing parallel turns.

Start in a steep traverse.

Keep facing downhill.

To stop, push your knees further into the hill to increase the edging of the skis.

Press your knees forwards and into the turn.

Press harder against your lower ski, and steer the turn with knee pressure forwards and into the hill.

Edge your skis.

The fan method

With practice, you will be able to begin this turn from steeper traverses until you are starting from a schuss. This is called the fan method. Stages 4 and 5 in this diagram are developed from the parallel uphill turn. Here the skier turns with parallel skis into and out of the fall line - steps 1-7 on the opposite page.

1 **2** **3** **4** **5**

Fall line

1 Turn out of a gentle traverse.
2 Turn out of a steep traverse.
3 Turn from a schuss.
4 Turn across fall line out of steep traverse.
5 Turn across fall line out of gentle traverse.

The stop swing

The stop swing is a method for stopping quickly, based on the parallel uphill turn. You stop by turning your skis around at right angles to the fall line and edging them strongly as shown below.

1 Begin by skiing down the fall line.

2 Rise up slightly to prepare for the turn.

3 Plant your inside pole and sink down and push your knees into the turn.

4 Edge your skis strongly until you come to a halt with your skis across the fall line.

The quicker you stop, the harder you need to press against your lower ski and the more you need to keep your head over it.

Parallel turns

Parallel turns are an efficient way of turning and will allow you to ski on most slopes and in most snow conditions*. In order to turn with your skis parallel, you need to unweight your skis momentarily, as described to the right.

Unweighting your skis

By a quick sinking or rising of your body, you can momentarily take the weight off your skis. This is called unweighting. Unweighting is an important part of turning because you can turn your skis with very little effort at the moment when they carry no weight.

The parallel turn shown below uses a rising movement to unweight the skis called up-unweighting.

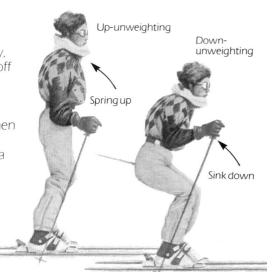

Up-unweighting

Down-unweighting

Spring up

Sink down

Parallel turn with up-unweighting

The simplest parallel turn is started by sinking down whilst planting the inside pole and then rising quickly and pushing your knees into the turn.

You will find it easier to turn if you are skiing at speed, so begin from position 4 in the fan method. Once you feel confident, try turning from a gentle traverse, position 5.

Start by skiing in a fairly steep traverse and bring your lower pole forwards ready to plant.

Sink down and plant your pole beside your lower ski, between the tip and boot.

Rise up quickly, pushing up on your pole, to unweight your skis, so that you can change edges.

Keep your shoulders and upper body tilting downhill, and bank your knees into the turn.

Ski positions

Traverse

Pole plant

Rise up — skis flat

Steering

Traverse

Skis edged

Fall line

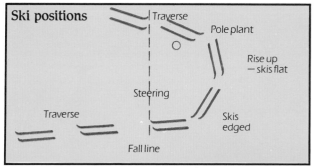

Your inside edges should bite into the snow as you continue steering the turn.

You will now be ready to try another parallel turn in the opposite direction.

When the turn is complete, lift the pole and continue in a traverse.

*See page 53 for more about different snow conditions.

17

More parallel turns and advanced schussing

Moguls

Moguls are bumps in the snow made by skiers. Many steep slopes are a maze of bumps and are known as mogul fields. They are built up as more and more skiers take the same route down a steep slope. When the skier turns, the skis carve out snow which is sprayed to the side. Each skier digs up more snow, causing deeper ruts and higher bumps.

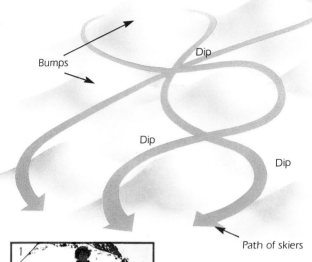

Bumps

Dip

Dip

Dip

Path of skiers

Skiing on moguls

As a beginner, mogul fields can appear to be quite frightening. For a more experienced skier, however, moguls can provide exciting skiing*.

The best technique to use for skiing down a mogul field is bending turning. This uses a technique called down-unweighting, rather than the up-unweighting used in the parallel turn on page 17. Here you can find out how to do bending turns, and how to use them on moguls.

Bending turning

Bending turns are easier to do if you are skiing at speed, so start from a steep traverse. As you approach the turn, bend your knees and then relax your leg muscles completely for an instant to unweight your skis, as shown to the right.

Begin in a traverse and bring your inside pole forwards ready to plant.

Plant your inside pole out to the side and continue to face down the fall line.

Begin the turn by relaxing your leg muscles and sinking down to unweight your skis.

Ski positions

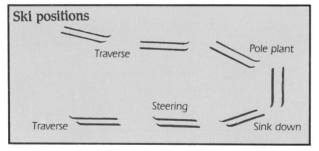

Traverse

Pole plant

Traverse

Steering

Sink down

Ski past the pole with your skis facing down the fall line.

Once the turn is complete, continue in a traverse, ready to begin another turn.

Push hard against your outside ski to edge it as you steer the turn.

Bank your knees into the turn, and steer the turn with your knees and feet.

*See page 47 for mogul competition skiing.

Bending turning on moguls

Moguls will help you begin a bending turn. If you ski to the top of one, you will feel your knees being pushed up towards your chest, so your body is already in the correct position to begin the turn.

Your skis turn easily on top of a bump because only a small area of them is in contact with the snow. When you push your thighs, knees and feet into the turn, your skis spin around your feet.

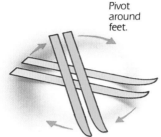

Pivot around feet.

As you ski up to a mogul, allow your legs to bend up to absorb the bump as you come up to the top.

Plant your inside pole sideways on the top of the mogul.

As you ski past the pole, relax your leg muscles and bank your knees into the turn.

A common mistake

Do not sit back over the tails of your skis when you bend to begin the turn. Your knees should be bent forwards and you should feel your ankles pushing against the front of your boots.

Stretch your legs sideways into the dip, and transfer your weight onto the outside ski.

Turn your skis by pushing your thighs, knees and feet into the turn.

Further useful techniques - advanced schussing

To schuss on steeper slopes, you use a different technique to that used for schussing on gentle slopes (see page 8). Lean forwards so that your body is always at right angles to the slope. Use the "egg position", shown far right, to lessen wind resistance and increase speed.

Slow schuss

Body upright, knees slightly bent.

Faster schuss

Bend further forwards, body at right angles to slope.

Increasing speed

Knees bent forwards over your skis and your body crouched down into the "egg position".

Schussing from a steep slope to flat ground

If the slope you are skiing down suddenly flattens out, ▶ you will be thrown forwards abruptly. This is because your skis suddenly slow down but your body continues to move forwards, as shown to the right.

Compensate for the change in slope by stretching your ▶ legs and leaning back slightly just before the slope flattens. Then bend your legs and crouch your body forwards to absorb the jolt.

This technique is also useful for coping with the sudden loss of speed experienced if you ski from a smooth piste into deep snow.

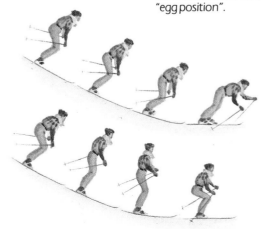

Lifts

Before ski lifts were invented, you had to climb uphill in order to ski down. People either carried their skis, or wore them with skins attached underneath to stop sliding backwards.

Today, all skiing resorts have lifts to carry or tow you quickly up the mountain. There are two main types of ski lift: those you ride with your skis on, and those you ride with your skis off. These are described here with tips on how to use them.

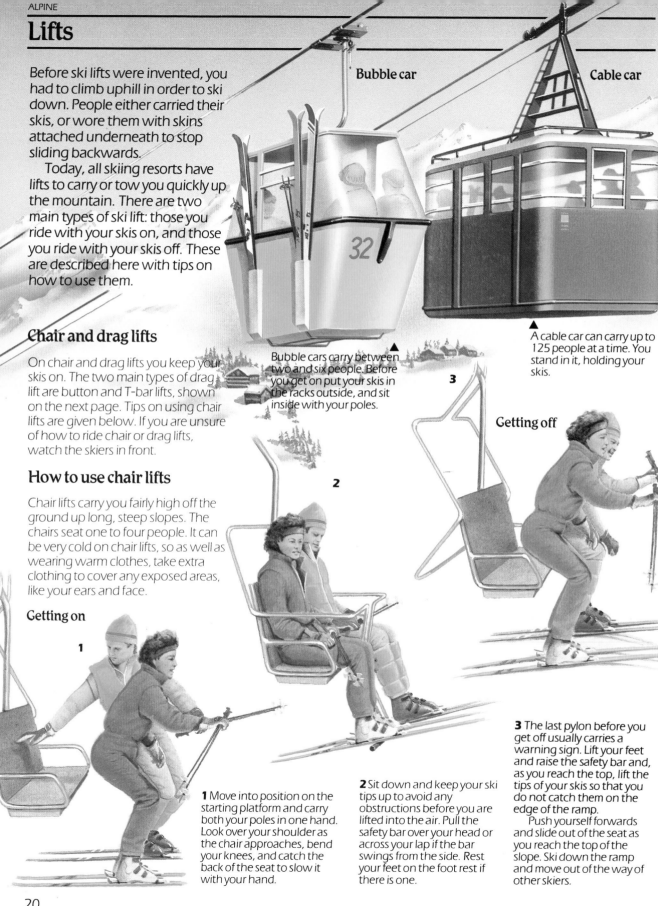

Bubble car

Cable car

A cable car can carry up to 125 people at a time. You stand in it, holding your skis.

Bubble cars carry between two and six people. Before you get on put your skis in the racks outside, and sit inside with your poles.

Chair and drag lifts

On chair and drag lifts you keep your skis on. The two main types of drag lift are button and T-bar lifts, shown on the next page. Tips on using chair lifts are given below. If you are unsure of how to ride chair or drag lifts, watch the skiers in front.

How to use chair lifts

Chair lifts carry you fairly high off the ground up long, steep slopes. The chairs seat one to four people. It can be very cold on chair lifts, so as well as wearing warm clothes, take extra clothing to cover any exposed areas, like your ears and face.

Getting on

Getting off

1 Move into position on the starting platform and carry both your poles in one hand. Look over your shoulder as the chair approaches, bend your knees, and catch the back of the seat to slow it with your hand.

2 Sit down and keep your ski tips up to avoid any obstructions before you are lifted into the air. Pull the safety bar over your head or across your lap if the bar swings from the side. Rest your feet on the foot rest if there is one.

3 The last pylon before you get off usually carries a warning sign. Lift your feet and raise the safety bar and, as you reach the top, lift the tips of your skis so that you do not catch them on the edge of the ramp.

Push yourself forwards and slide out of the seat as you reach the top of the slope. Ski down the ramp and move out of the way of other skiers.

20

How to use a T-bar lift

A T-bar lift is an inverted wooden "T" on the end of a spring-loaded wire attached to moving cable which runs up and down the slope in a continuous loop. T-bar lifts are designed to tow two people up a slope in a straight line, although you can go on your own.

It is much easier to ride a T-bar with two people as you balance each other. Choose a partner about the same height as you. Take care to keep your skis parallel. Lean in towards each other to avoid crossing skis with your partner.

Getting on

Stand in the starting area with your skis parallel and both poles in one hand.

Watch over your shoulder for the T-bar and catch it with your inside hand.

Pull the arm of the "T" down and lodge it under your bottom - don't sit.

Hold the bar in one hand and bend your knees ready for the starting jerk.

Getting off

As you arrive at the top of the lift, pull the bar down and slip it to one side behind you, as shown to the right. One of you should let go first, leaving the other to let the bar go gently. Ski away to one side to keep out of the way of the next skiers.

How to use a button lift

Button lifts are similar to T-bars, except they only take one person and can change direction. Instead of the "T", there is a pole with a disk, or button at the end.

Getting on

Getting off

Get into position, skis parallel and both poles in one hand, and grab the bar.

Pull the bar down and slip the button between your legs, behind your bottom.

Do not sit on the button. Bend your knees slightly to absorb the starting jerk.

Pull the bar down, slip the button from between your legs and gently let it go.

Tips on riding drag lifts

* On steep sections of the path, bend your knees more and lean further forwards to keep your balance.

* Occasionally the path will slope downhill. Push your skis into a slight snowplough to slow down.

* If you go across bumps and dips, bend your knees at the top of the bumps and stretch them in the dips (see page 8).

* If you fall off, let go of the bar and move to the side as quickly as possible, out of the way of following skiers.

Types of ski and how they are made

Successful skiing depends on using the correct skis, boots, bindings and poles. You can rent these items at skiing resorts. Hire shops are usually able to give expert advice on choosing the correct equipment. If you decide to ski regularly it may be worth buying your own equipment. Make sure you get expert advice from the ski shop before you buy.

Types of ski

There are many different types of ski, but most fit into the three categories below.

Most skiers use ▶ standard recreational skis. These can be used in most snow conditions for downhill skiing at slow speeds, and for shallow turns. Their length depends on the skier's ability, height and weight (see page 24).

◀ Racing and high performance skis are longer than recreational skis, which makes them more stable at high speeds. They go faster but are more difficult to turn at slow speeds than shorter skis. The side-cut (see right), length and flexibility depend on the event they are designed for. Some have aerodynamic holes in the tip for downhill and super giant slalom events*.

Some beginners start ▶ on very short skis and build up to full length skis day by day as they learn. This is a teaching method called Ski Evolotiv.

Short skis skid well and help beginners learn how to turn.

Parts of a ski

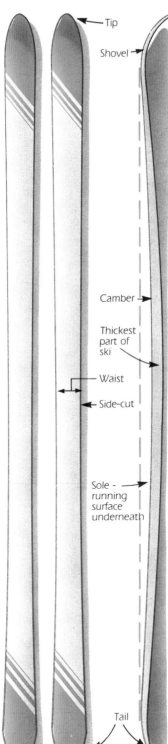

- Tip
- Shovel
- Camber
- Thickest part of ski
- Waist
- Side-cut
- Sole - running surface underneath
- Tail

The pictures on the left show the basic features of an ordinary recreational ski. Specialized skis have the same features but vary in length, side-cut and flexibility. You can find out how skis are designed to help performance on page 60.

Ski sides are curved inwards. This is called a "side-cut" and the thinnest part is called the waist.

A ski is thicker in the centre than at the tip and tail, and has an upward curve, called a camber. When you stand on a ski the curve is pressed down flat, spreading your weight evenly over the whole ski.

Skis vary in the amount they flex. A more flexible ski is good for skiing on soft snow and for ordinary skiers. A less flexible ski is good for hard snow and ice, and for expert ski control.

Edges

Skis have steel edges along each side to help the ski to grip the snow and turn. It is important to keep them sharp (see page 25) to reduce skidding on hard snow.

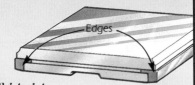

Edges

Ski twist

The amount of twist in a ski, called "torsional rigidity", varies according to the type of ski and is needed to help transmit the tilting movement of the leg and boot to the front and back of the ski. Heavy and expert skiers need more ridigity to keep their edges in contact with the snow.

Skis twist like this.

* See pages 37 and 40.

How skis are made

Skis were once made of solid wood. Today all skis have plastic tops, polyethylene running surfaces, steel edges, and cores which are usually made from layers of wood or foam plastic. The cores of some skis are within a fibreglass beam, called a torsion box. The torsion box helps to control the ski's flexibility. Some different kinds of core make-up are shown below.

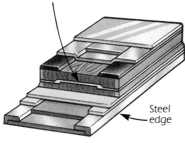
Laminated wood core

Steel edge

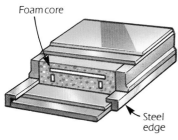
Foam core

Steel edge

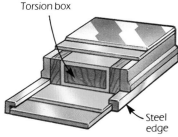
Torsion box

Steel edge

In a ski factory the components of a ski are bonded in a mould, under high pressure and heat for 20 minutes. It is then ready for finishing. This involves many stages of grinding, printing and lacquering or varnishing.

Specialized skiing

There are some special skis, different from recreational and racing skis, which are used for special types of skiing. The pictures below show some of these and the equipment that goes with them.

Mono-skiers use one ▶ wide ski which holds both boots side by side. Mono-skis are especially good for off-piste skiing as they "float" well in deep snow. They are also good for skiing in soupy snow* on-piste.

◀ Snow-surfers use a wide deck, like a small surf board, with boot straps or fixed shells to secure their feet with. They surf and jump over ridges and cornices and slide through gulleys, as if they were surfing waves.

Grass skis have ▶ caterpillar tracks underneath for skiing down grass slopes. The tracks are well lubricated so that they can go very fast. Grass skiers hold their own slalom and downhill racing competitions.

◀ Parachutes can be used to pull skiers uphill in areas where there are no lifts. The parachute is steered with ropes that pull the skier. At the top of the slope, the parachute is deflated and carried on the skier's back for the downhill run.

Ski-sailing is done with a ▶ windsurfing sail linked to the skis. The skier angles the sail to catch the wind. Ski sailing is done in flat, wide open, windy spaces such as snow covered lakes.

See page 53 for different snow conditions

Choosing skis and ski maintenance

Whether you rent or buy skis, it is important that they are suitable for your height, weight, ability and the kind of skiing you want to do. These two pages give advice on how to choose skis, including tips on buying second hand, and advice on how to look after them.

Length of ski

Use the score card below to work out what length of ski you need. It is based on your skiing ability, the kind of skiing you like to do and your height. It assumes average weight for your height.

Choose one option from sections A, B and C, and note down your points for each.

HOW WELL DO YOU SKI?	POINTS
You are a nervous beginner	10
You are an enthusiastic beginner	12
You have just learnt how to ski parallel	15
You ski parallel at a slow, easy pace	18
You ski confidently at moderate speeds on red runs	22
You enjoy black slopes but are not yet very confident on them	28
You are learning to turn continuously on mogul slopes	31
You are fast and confident on all slopes	33
You are fast and expert on all slopes	35
SELECT ONE AND NOTE YOUR POINTS (A)	e.g.12

WHERE DO YOU LIKE TO SKI?	
On easy pisted slopes	5
On moderate pisted slopes	8
On moguls and powder	10
On all slopes	13
On fast open slopes - racing	15
SELECT ONE AND NOTE YOUR POINTS (B)	e.g.8

WHAT IS YOUR HEIGHT?	
100cm	70
110cm	80
120cm	90
130cm	100
140cm	110
150cm	120
160cm	130
170cm	140
180cm and over	150
NOTE YOUR POINTS (C)	e.g.90

Add up the points for A, B and C. The total score is the length of ski you need in centimetres. Round the figure to the nearest manufactured length. If you are a bit heavy for your height add 5 or 10cm. If you are very light, subtract 5cm.

Flexible or stiff skis?

The amount of flex and twist you need in a ski will depend on your skiing ability, where you like to ski and your weight. In general, if you are an expert or heavy skier you will need a stiffer ski than beginners. It is a good idea to ask your ski shop for advice.

Choosing second-hand skis

There are second-hand skis for sale in most ski resorts. If you are a keen beginner it may be sensible to buy second-hand to begin with as you will probably want to change them for longer skis within a year or two. Find out the length you need by using the score card on the left and use the checks below to see if the skis are in good condition.

* Make sure that the edges have not pulled away from the sides of the ski.

* Check that the edges are sharp by scraping the back of your fingernail against them. If you get a good shaving the edge is sharp.

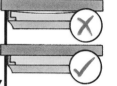

* Check that the soles of the skis are flat by holding a ruler against them, particularly under the bindings. If you can see light under the ruler, the sole is worn and the ski will not turn properly.

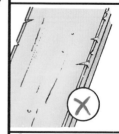

* It is best to examine skis unwaxed as wax will fill in and cover up gaps. Look out for large grooves in the sole, particularly next to the edges as they will affect how the ski turns. You can easily repair small gooves yourself as shown on the next page.

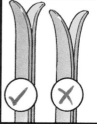

* Squeeze both skis together, sole to sole, to check whether they are bent. They should diverge from each other just below the shovels. If they diverge further down, they are bent and will not keep contact with the snow properly.

Maintaining your skis

Make sure that your skis always have smooth, flat soles, sharp square edges and well-waxed running surfaces. If your skis are in poor condition your skiing will be affected. You can maintain your skis and repair minor damage yourself, as shown below.

Flattening soles

In time ski soles wear down. Check for this by doing the ruler test, described on the previous page. If the soles are not too badly worn, flatten them with a coarse flat file.

Grip the file with both hands and press down hard as you work it diagonally across the ski from tip to tail, as shown below.

Press down hard on the file.

Filling soles

You can repair shallow notches in the sole by using a special "candle" made of a plastic/wax mixture, which you can buy to match the colour of your soles. Light the candle with a gas flame and drip the mixture into the holes. Leave it to set according to the manufacturer's instructions and then scrape the surface smooth. You can buy special scrapers to do this.

Deep notches which expose the material beneath the sole should be repaired by experts in a ski shop.

Hold candle close and keep flame small and blue.

Scraper

Sharpening edges

It is important to keep the edges sharp by filing them with a special right-angled file. For even sharper edges you can use files angled up to 85°.

Run the file along the edge of the ski. It is sharp enough if it will shave the back of your fingernail (see earlier test).

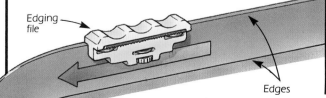

Edging file

Edges

Waxing

Waxing the soles of your skis decreases friction between the running surface and the snow, so that they glide more easily. Wax also protects soles.

You can buy special waxes for different snow conditions. Cold snow crystals are spiky and require a hard wax, and snow at around melting point (e.g. "spring snow"), requires a softer wax. You can also buy a universal wax for general use.

Applying wax

There are several ways of applying wax: you can rub it in, use aerosol or tube waxes or use a method called "hot waxing". Hot waxing is the best method as it lasts well and the heat enables the wax to enter tiny pores in the ski.

Hot waxing

For hot waxing you need an ordinary non-steam iron or you can buy a special ski waxer (which is also useful for filling in small grooves or notches).

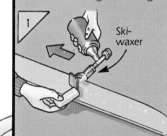

Ski-waxer

1

Make sure that the ski sole is clean. Hold a stick of wax against a hot ski-waxer or iron and drip 20-30 blobs of melted wax up the middle of the sole (or each side of the running groove if your ski has one).

Iron the wax evenly into the ski, moving the iron all the time. Do not stop the iron on one part of the ski, as you could damage it. Leave the wax to harden for a few minutes.

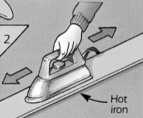

2

Hot iron

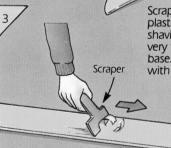

3

Scraper

Scrape off excess wax with a plastic scraper until no more shavings appear, to leave a very thin film of wax on the base. Rub down the sole with a soft cloth.

The harder the snow is, the sooner the wax will wear off. As a general rule, re-apply stick, aerosol and tube wax each day, and hot wax once or twice a week.

Boots, bindings and poles

Ski boots

Ski boots link your body to your skis and are the most important items of skiing equipment. Good boots are needed so that you can transfer force from your legs to your skis and control your direction. Boots also support your ankles and keep your feet warm and comfortable. Like skis, there are many different types of boots to suit your skiing ability.

How boots are constructed

All boots have a rigid plastic outer shell which is angled forward and a hinge at the ankle to make forward movement comfortable. They have various adjustments at the back or side which can be altered to make the boot fit tightly across the heel and across the foot. Inside the outer shell is a soft, removable, inner boot made of foam, lined with fabric. You can buy boots that have the inner boot injected with foam whilst your foot is in it so that it fits you perfectly.

The three main types of boot are shown below.

Beginner

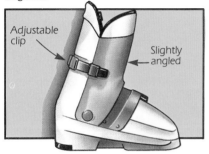

This is a typical beginner's boot which is only slightly angled forward. It is a "rear-entry" boot, opening from behind with an adjustable clip across the back to keep the boot tight.

Intermediate

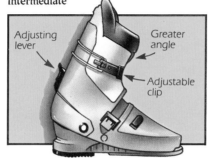

This is a more advanced rear entry boot for intermediate skiers. It is angled further forward and, in addition to the adjustable clip, has a lever at the back for adjusting the tightness of the boot around the foot.

Expert

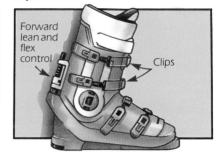

Advanced skiers and racers use tighter, more rigid boots. This is a "front-entry" boot with four front clips. It has a pronounced forward lean and many adjustable features to ensure a close fit.

Trying on boots

When you try on ski boots (either to hire or buy) wear one pair of socks long enough to reach above the cuff of the boot (the shop may provide a pair). Walk around in the boots for at least 15 minutes. They should feel comfortable, with no tightness or rubbing. The diagram below shows some points to look out for.

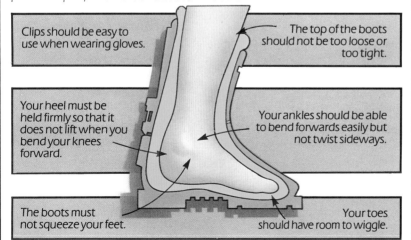

Clips should be easy to use when wearing gloves.

The top of the boots should not be too loose or too tight.

Your heel must be held firmly so that it does not lift when you bend your knees forward.

Your ankles should be able to bend forwards easily but not twist sideways.

The boots must not squeeze your feet.

Your toes should have room to wiggle.

Boot hints

* If you do not stand straight, there are boots with a built-in "canting" adjustment to compensate, or an inner sole can be fitted in normal boots to straighten your stance.

* If your boots are uncomfortable, take them back to the shop and ask for advice. Inner soles and foam padding can be fitted to help your boot fit properly, and some boot inners can be ground down to relieve pressure points.

* If you suffer from very cold feet, you can buy heated boots.

* Store boots with the clips done up, to help keep their shape.

* Never leave your boots near direct heat. Take out the inner boot if you need to dry it.

Bindings

Ski bindings are designed to clamp boots firmly onto skis but to release them in bad falls so that you do not injure your legs. The point at which bindings release is controlled by tension adjustments.

A binding usually has a separate heel and toe piece, as shown in the big picture below. The pieces are set to fit your boot size when you buy or hire bindings.

In a twisting fall, the toe piece lets the boot out sideways, and in a forwards fall, the heel piece releases to let the boot out forwards, as shown below.

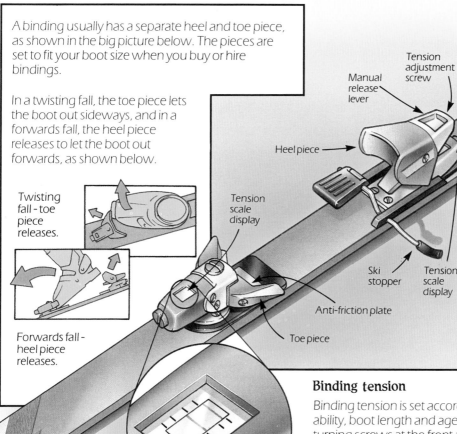

Twisting fall - toe piece releases.

Forwards fall - heel piece releases.

Manual release lever

Tension adjustment screw

Heel piece

Tension scale display

Ski stopper

Tension scale display

Anti-friction plate

Toe piece

Tension display

Ski stoppers

Ski stoppers (see left) are small spring-loaded brakes on bindings. When the binding is in the open position the brakes spring down and stick into the snow, stopping your ski from sliding down the slope. Some skis have safety straps instead, as shown below.

Strap

Safety straps do up round your ankles. If your skis come off in a fall they will still be attached to you by the straps. These are useful in powder snow* where skis can be lost.

Binding tension

Binding tension is set according to your weight, skiing ability, boot length and age. The tension is adjusted by turning screws at the front and back of the bindings. The setting is displayed in a small indicator on a scale from 1 to 20. Beginners start with a low setting; faster skiers use a high setting. Have your bindings fitted and tension set and checked regularly by an expert.

Ski poles

You need poles to help balance, turn and walk on skis. Poles are made of a strong, lightweight material such as aluminium, with steel tips and a plastic hand grip.

The most common type of hand grip is shown here. It has finger indents and a hand strap with safety poppers which come undone in a fall.

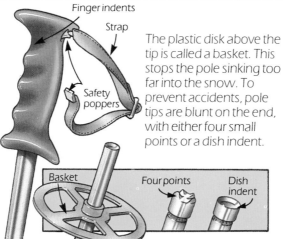

Finger indents

Strap

Safety poppers

Basket

Four points

Dish indent

The plastic disk above the tip is called a basket. This stops the pole sinking too far into the snow. To prevent accidents, pole tips are blunt on the end, with either four small points or a dish indent.

Choosing your poles

Your poles need to be the correct height for you to be able to use them properly.

To check that they are the correct height, hold the pole upside down just below the basket.

Keep your elbow against your side and rest the grip on the ground. Your forearm should be parallel to the ground.

Soft, deep snow.

Cross-country equipment and waxes

Cross-country skiing is rather like hiking on skis - either through unmarked countryside, called touring, or on prepared tracks, which you can find out about over the page.

It involves different techniques from alpine skiing because of the need to climb uphill and ski over large flat areas as well as skiing downhill. You ski on long, thin skis, in light boots attached to the bindings at the toe only - so that you can lift your heels.

Skis

Cross-country skis are designed both to grip the snow and glide forwards. They are divided into three zones: two for gliding and one for gripping, as shown below.

The camber is shaped so that the skier's weight is either on the grip or the glide zones, depending on whether their weight is on one or both skis.

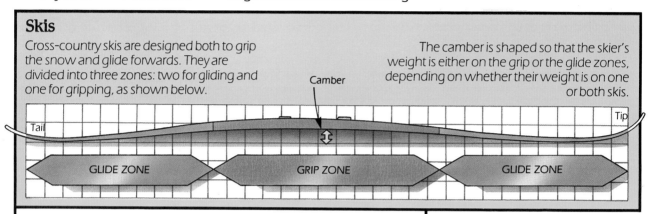

Camber

Tail · Tip

GLIDE ZONE · GRIP ZONE · GLIDE ZONE

Gliding

When standing with equal weight ▶ on both skis, when schussing, for example, the centre of the skis, the grip zone, only just touches the ground. All your weight is carried on the gliding zones at the front and back of the skis.

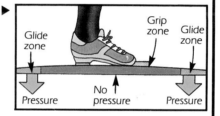

Glide zone · Grip zone · Glide zone

Pressure · No pressure · Pressure

Gripping

When most of your weight is on ▶ one ski (e.g. when walking) your weight presses down on the centre of the ski - the grip zone.

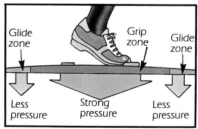

Glide zone · Grip zone · Glide zone

Less pressure · Strong pressure · Less pressure

How the grip zone works

The bases of cross-country skis are treated in a special way so that the grip zone grips the snow and the glide zones allow the skis to glide forwards freely. There are two types of skis: those which need gripping and gliding wax, and skis with a special built-in base, called "no-wax" skis.

No-wax skis

The base of no-wax skis is grooved in such a way that they can slide forwards freely but cannot slide back. These skis are particularly suitable for beginners as they can be used in all weather conditions without lengthy waxing.

Two common types of bases are shown below.

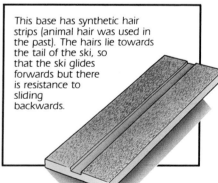

This base has synthetic hair strips (animal hair was used in the past). The hairs lie towards the tail of the ski, so that the ski glides forwards but there is resistance to sliding backwards.

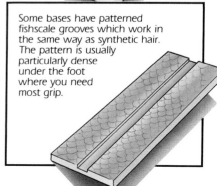

Some bases have patterned fishscale grooves which work in the same way as synthetic hair. The pattern is usually particularly dense under the foot where you need most grip.

Choosing skis

* To find the right ski length for you, stand with your arm stretched above your head. The tip of the ski should reach to about the palm of your hand.

* For touring, it is best to buy skis with a side-cut (like Alpine skis) which will help you turn on downhill runs.

* For cross-country races (see pages 44-45), buy skis with a stiff camber. This reduces the ski's contact with the snow and helps them to glide faster, although a harder kick is needed to engage the wax in the grip zone.

Waxable skis

Waxable skis work in the same way as no-wax skis, but waxes are used to provide the correct amount of grip and glide. You need to apply a glide wax to the gliding zones, and grip wax to the grip zone.

The wax you use depends on the temperature and snow conditions. Glide waxes are similar to those used on alpine skis (see page 25) and they come in a colour coded range according to different conditions. There are two main types of grip waxes: hard for cold, dry conditions and soft for soupy warm conditions. Within these types there are a range of waxes which are also colour coded. A typical wax coding chart is shown on the right.

Temperature	+1°	0°		−1°	−7°
Snow conditions	Wet soupy snow	Wet soupy snow to colder snow, large crystals		Moderately cold, dry snow – hard crust or new snow	Cold, dry snow, small fine crystals
Specialized waxes Glide zone	Red glider	Violet glider		Blue glider	Green glider
Grip zone	Red klister	Red wax / Violet wax / Violet klister	Silver klister / Yellow klister	Blue wax / Blue klister	Green wax / Green klister
Glide zone	Red glider	Violet glider		Blue glider	Green glider
General waxes		Plus	Minus	Beginners can use a two-wax system for grip waxes: one for temperatures above 0°C and one for temperature below 0°.	

Applying wax

Scrape off any old wax and wipe the ski with solvent applied with a rag. Make sure your skis are dry before applying new wax. Apply the wax sparingly, following the manufacturer's instructions.

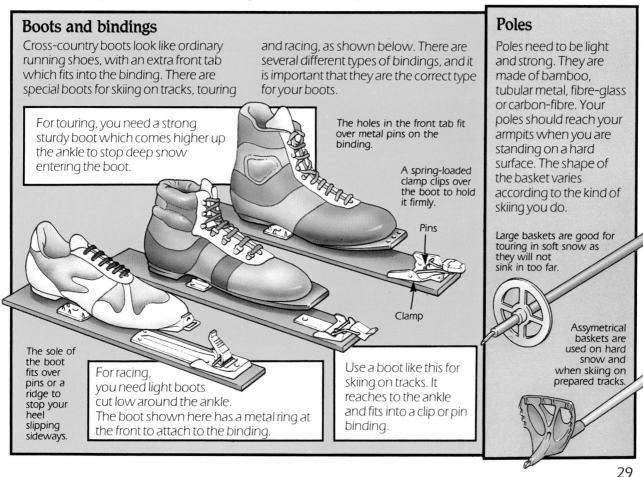

Boots and bindings

Cross-country boots look like ordinary running shoes, with an extra front tab which fits into the binding. There are special boots for skiing on tracks, touring and racing, as shown below. There are several different types of bindings, and it is important that they are the correct type for your boots.

For touring, you need a strong sturdy boot which comes higher up the ankle to stop deep snow entering the boot.

The holes in the front tab fit over metal pins on the binding.

A spring-loaded clamp clips over the boot to hold it firmly.

Pins

Clamp

The sole of the boot fits over pins or a ridge to stop your heel slipping sideways.

For racing, you need light boots cut low around the ankle. The boot shown here has a metal ring at the front to attach to the binding.

Use a boot like this for skiing on tracks. It reaches to the ankle and fits into a clip or pin binding.

Poles

Poles need to be light and strong. They are made of bamboo, tubular metal, fibre-glass or carbon-fibre. Your poles should reach your armpits when you are standing on a hard surface. The shape of the basket varies according to the kind of skiing you do.

Large baskets are good for touring in soft snow as they will not sink in too far.

Assymetrical baskets are used on hard snow and when skiing on prepared tracks.

Skiing on tracks

The basics of cross-country skiing are simple and easy to learn. When you begin, it is best to use the specially prepared tracks found in many skiing resorts. The tracks are made by machines which press new snow into a firm surface whilst cutting out parallel grooves for the skis. The tracks will help you keep your skis together so you only have to think about moving forwards.

Once you have learnt the basic techniques shown here, you may want to tour into the country and make your own tracks. To ski downhill on cross-country skis you use much the same techniques as in Alpine skiing, except for the telemark turn. You can find out about this on page 33.

Walking and gliding

The first thing you need to learn is how to walk and glide naturally and easily. This is much easier on cross-country skis than on alpine skis as the skis are light and the bindings allow you to lift your heel.

To walk on cross-country skis, push off with one foot and the opposite pole and glide the other foot forward. Then do the same with your other foot and pole. Once you have mastered an easy walking rhythm you will be able to speed up into a fast glide.

Turning from stationary

The clock turn, described on page 7, is the simplest way of turning on the spot on level ground. The kick turn is the best technique if you want to turn through 180° across the fall line.

The kick turn

The kick turn, shown to the right, is a good exercise for improving your balance as well as being a useful turn to learn.

Plant your right pole level with your left foot. Push off with your pole and left foot.

Start by standing with your skis at right angles to the fall line and your poles on either side of you.

Walking uphill

You can walk up gentle slopes on cross-country skis because the non-slip base or wax on the bottom of the skis give some grip.

If your skis start to slide back, change to the herringbone or, on steep slopes, use the side-step*.

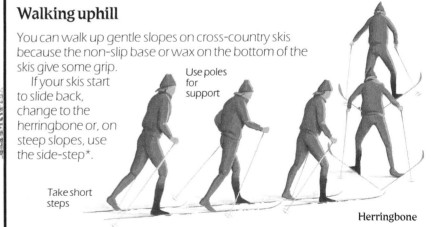

Use poles for support

Take short steps

Herringbone

Double-pole push

You can go faster on fairly flat ground by keeping your skis together and pushing off from both poles at once, as shown on the right.

You can also combine the double-pole push with a single leg kick off. Here you use both poles as leverage as you glide forwards on alternate legs, having kicked off with the other.

Skis parallel.

Plant poles.

*The herringbone and side-stepping are explained on page 6.

A common mistake

Glide forwards on your right ski and bring your left pole forwards, ready to plant.

Plant your left pole level with your right foot and push off, gliding on your left ski.

Continue, with your right arm and left leg working together and your left arm with your right leg.

If you ski with stiff knees, as shown above, your hips will be stiff and you will not be able to glide.

Put your weight on your upper ski and kick your lower ski into the air in front of you.

Stretch out your leg to bring the ski vertical. Lift your lower pole and plant it behind you uphill.

Lean back onto your poles and pivot the vertical ski around on its tail. Place it next to the upper ski.

With your weight on the lower ski, lift your upper ski round parallel to the lower ski.

Skating steps and turns

Skating steps are used for turning as well as for increasing speed when you ski on tracks. The basic technique is to stand on one ski and push with the other at an angle to the side of the track. It is similar to using a push-scooter.

Side-step

Turns

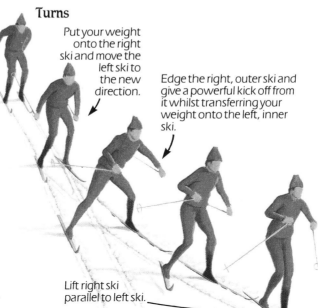

Put your weight onto the right ski and move the left ski to the new direction.

Edge the right, outer ski and give a powerful kick off from it whilst transferring your weight onto the left, inner ski.

Lift right ski parallel to left ski.

Steps

Ski angled

Keep one foot in the track and step your other ski outside at an angle.

Push off

Plant your poles next to your feet and push off from the angled ski.

Push down on poles.

31

Cross-country touring

Cross-country skiing began in Scandinavia where, although there are a few specially prepared tracks, many cross-country skiers tour open countryside. Cross-country touring is becoming more and more popular in the snowy parts of the world.

Tours can take a few hours or several days. You need to plan carefully, especially for unmarked routes. It is important to follow the mountain rules below for safe, enjoyable touring.

The mountain rules

1 Don't go for long trips unless you are fit.

2 Always tell someone where you are going and when you expect to return.

3 Look at the weather and listen to forecasts before leaving.

4 Don't be a know-all - listen to people more experienced than you.

5 Storms can occur even on short trips. Take a rucksack with the equipment you will need (see below).

6 NEVER forget your map and compass.

7 NEVER go alone.

8 If you are less than half-way to your destination by mid-day, turn back home.

9 Seek shelter in time, if necessary, or dig in (see opposite page) to conserve your energy and get out of the wind.

Equipment for a long day tour

You need to take the things shown in the checklist below. Some items are included in case you need to stay out overnight in an emergency. It is best to carry them in a close-fitting rucksack which does not restrict your movement when skiing. Split the equipment between the people you are touring with so that no one has a heavy load to carry.

Checklist

Food

You need carbohydrates for energy (e.g. in chocolate and sandwiches). Oranges are refreshing when you stop for a rest. Take a water bottle, a kettle and a small spirit or gas stove to brew hot drinks.

Clothes

It is best to wear several loose layers of clothing, with wool or cotton next to your skin. This allows your body to release heat after climbing, as well as protecting against damp and cold. Take extra socks, mittens, hat, goggles and a wind-proof jacket.

Safety equipment

Snow shovel (plastic), safety rope, matches and wax candle, map, compass, pocket flashlight and a whistle to attract attention in case you are injured. Take an insulated mat and a sleeping bag in case you have to dig in. You can also use the sleeping bag for wrapping up casualties if necessary.

First aid

Take a simple kit including plasters for blisters.

Repair equipment

Swiss army knife, screwdriver, spare screws and parts for bindings, spare ski tip and waxes.

Touring technique

On cross-country tours you will need to be able to climb uphill, ski downhill and turn, as well as ski on flat ground. The telemark turn, shown below, is a special cross-country turn which is very useful when skiing downhill in powder snow.

Telemark turn

The telemark turn is only possible to do on cross-country skis as you need to lift your heels. The low turning position is stable, allowing you to move your weight back and forth to ski over bumps and hollows.

Begin by gliding your outside ski in front of the inside ski, bending your inside knee low.

Use your poles for balance.

Bring the outside ski forward so your foot is next to the tip of the inside ski.

Angle the outside ski into the turn. Edge it by bending your knee into the hill.

Once the turn is complete, bring the new upper ski back parallel with the other ski.

Digging in

Digging a snow hole can be fun close to home, but you may need one for survival; to stay dry and, more importantly, keep out of the wind, if you are stranded at nightfall. There are several ways of digging in, from holes in a drift to igloos. Two basic shelters are shown here, though it is advisable to learn from experts how to build safe shelters.

Points to remember:

1 Make sure there is always a hole to let in air. Keep a ski pole in the hole and take turns throughout the night to move it around the sides of the hole to make sure it is not blocked with snow.

2 Burn a candle - whilst it is alight there is oxygen in the air. Check it regularly throughout the night. If it goes out, leave the shelter as the oxygen has run out.

3 Build a ledge to sleep on and a hollow, or sink, below the ledge and entrance. The sink traps cold air, leaving the ledge warmer.

4 Place a pair of upright skis outside your shelter so people can see where you are.

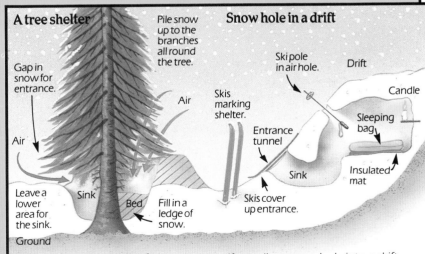

A tree shelter

Pile snow up to the branches all round the tree.

Gap in snow for entrance.

Air

Air

Leave a lower area for the sink.

Sink

Bed

Fill in a ledge of snow.

Ground

Snow hole in a drift

Ski pole in air hole.

Drift

Candle

Skis marking shelter.

Entrance tunnel

Sleeping bag

Sink

Insulated mat

Skis cover up entrance.

The fanning branches of an evergreen tree make a good shelter as there is usually a hollow in the snow beneath the branches. Pile snow up to the branches to keep out wind.

If you dig a snow hole into a drift, choose your site very carefully. Steep or overhanging slopes may avalanche, so choose a drift in a gentle slope. Dig the hole with a shovel or your skis.

Events and history

The next 14 pages give an outline of the main skiing events - how they are structured and judged and special techniques that are used.

Competition skiing is divided into three groups: alpine, nordic and freestyle. Alpine events include gaint slalom, supergiant slalom, slalom and downhill racing; nordic events include ski jumping, cross-countgry racing and biathlon events; and freestyle, the newest discipline, includes aerials, mogul racing and ballet.

How competition began

The world's first ski event was held in Norway in 1866 at Christiania (now called Oslo). It began when a man called Elling Baekken came to Christiania and challenged the local skiers to match their skills against his. He demonstrated his downhill, jumping and cross-country skiing talents. The next year, Elling Baekken was invited to return to a properly organized competition which included cross-country and downhill, with jumps in the downhill event.

Norheim* took part in the competition in 1868, and won with his revolutionary equipment and skills.

Twenty years later, the Finns discovered that two poles were better than one for cross-country skiing - a radical change in equipment.

In 1892, the competition was transferred to Holmenkollen, Norway, with just two events: jumping and cross-country. This competition is still held in Holmenkollen today.

Alpine competition

Downhill racing, which began as a Nordic event, became popular in Switzerland in 1902. At first there were no set rules, and the winner was the first to ski from the top of the mountain to a set finish line.

Early downhill race.

Zdarsky, the Austrian who invented the stem turn*, was insistent that safety should come first in skiing. He introduced gates in downhill courses to slow down the skiers' speeds. In 1905, Zdarsky staged an event in Lilienfield which was similar to the giant slalom of today. There were 85 gates over a drop of 489m.

Mathias Zdarsky

Other events in the area followed this, but there were no more gate races until 1922, when Arnold Lunn, from Britain, set a slalom course in Murren, Switzerland. He decided to organize a competition as part of the Alpine Challenge Cup (an early competition series) which would test the skiers' ability to turn, but that would be judged on speed. He set flags in pairs down the slope, and the skiers were timed as they raced through them. This was the beginning of modern slalom skiing.

Arnold Lunn at Murren.

 * See page 55 for more on Norheim and Zdarsky

International Ski Federation

As the interest in skiing grew, there was a need for an overall governing body. The Federation Internationale de Ski (abbreviated to F.I.S.) was formed in 1924. The first international combined downhill and slalom races were held in the same year.

The F.I.S. is still responsible today for international regulations and safety standards.

The main competitions

The three main events in the skiing calendar are the Olympics, World Championships and the World Cup.

World Championships

There have been annual World Championships in cross-country racing since 1925.

The first World Championships in slalom and downhill were held at Murren, Switzerland in 1931, organized by the Ski Club of Great Britain.

World Championships are now held every two years. They are divided into alpine, nordic and freestyle. The events are held at different skiing resorts around the world within the skiing season.

Olympics

The first Winter Olympics were held in Chamonix, France in 1924.

The Olympics are held every four years, but not in the same years as World Championship events. The calendar works as follows:

1984 - Olympics
1985 - World Championships
1986 - free year
1987 - World Championships
1988 - Olympics
1989 - World Championships
1990 - free year
1991 - World Championships
1992 - Olympics

In the Winter Olympics, all the different skiing events are held together in one place and other sports are included such as bobsleigh, skating and ice-hockey.

World Cup

The World Cup was introduced in 1967 and happens every year. There are a series of individual races in each event throughout the skiing season. Points are awarded for each race, and at the end of the season a cup is awarded to the overall winner of each event.

A World Cup is also awarded for a combination of events - the winner must have achieved points in at least two of the alpine events at specially nominated races.

Other competitions

Other events in the skiing calendar include the European Cup series, ordinary international championships and national championships.

Giant and supergiant slalom

There are three types of slalom event in competition skiing: giant slalom, supergiant slalom and slalom. You can find out about these over the next four pages.

Giant slalom

Giant slalom combines some of the speed and excitement of downhill racing while also demanding nimble, fast turns. It is considered by experts to be the most physically, technically and athletically demanding alpine event.

The timing begins when the skier passes through the starting gate.

Starting order

The starting order in the first run is worked out according to the number of points competitors have accumulated in previous F.I.S. events. The highest ranked skiers go first.

In the second run, the five fastest competitors in the first run go first in reverse order - the fifth-fastest first, then the fourth-fastest - and so on. The fastest skier in the first run has the advantage of knowing what times to beat.

The starting order for giant slalom is also the same for the other slalom events.

The skier is allowed to knock a gate pole, but both skis must pass through the gate. There are judges by each gate to check that they do.

Section of a giant slalom course

Open gates

Closed gates

Key
Two possible routes through gates.

The course

The course is laid out to allow the competitor to ski it in a flowing manner whilst at the same time testing a variety of techniques.

There are strict F.I.S. rules governing course preparation. Excessively sharp ridges, ledges that would cause the skier to leave the ground for long distances and hidden obstacles, must be removed. There must be enough turning gates to limit the skier to a safe speed. The snow must be as hard as possible and if snow falls during the race, it must be removed or compacted.

Each course must have a drop of 250-400 metres in men's events, 250-350 metres in women's events, with a minimum drop of 300 metres for both sexes in World Cup events. The course should also be hilly.

The number of gates in each course must be within 12-15% of the vertical drop in metres. For example, a course with a 400 metre drop must have 48 to 60 gates. There should be both single gates and chicanes of multiple gates.

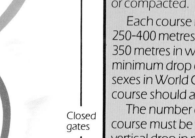

Open gate — 75cm
Closed gate — 30cm

The gates can be "open" - that is, positioned horizontally across the fall line - or "closed" - that is lying along the fall line (see left). They must be 4-8m wide with a minimum distance between them of 10m.

Each gate consists of two pairs of poles, each pair linked to a banner. The poles for closed gates are 30cm apart and 75cm apart for open gates.

The race

Before the race, competitors slide alongside the course to study it, but they are not allowed to ski the course itself. The course is then skied by non-competing "forerunners" who mark the path through the gates.

Competitors are judged on two electronically timed runs, done on different courses. Times for both runs are added, and the winner is the one with the shortest overall time.

Giant slalom technique

The skier has to select and follow the best line through the gates, minimize the amount of braking on each turn and accelerate as much as possible between turns.

Low fast position

Because of the high speed of giant slalom, skiers maintain a low stance most of the time and make gentle, rounded turns by steering with their legs and rarely using their poles.

Disqualification

Competitors are disqualified if they receive assistance on the course or do not pass through a gate properly. They can finish on one ski if the other is lost. If disqualified, a competitor cannot continue or go into the second run.

Supergiant slalom

Supergiant slalom, or Super-G, first appeared in the World Cup, amid controversy, in the 1982/3 season. It was intended to be an event even closer to downhill (see page 40) than giant slalom. The course is steeper and has more widely spaced gates than giant slalom, making it a much faster race.

Some people were worried that its inclusion in World Cup events would make the competitors even more specialized, but others looked forward to seeing competitors win prizes in both Super-G and downhill racing.

The skier goes over a ridge and takes off into the air.

The course

Skiers compete over one course only. The drop is much greater than in a giant slalom course: 500-600 metres for men and 350-500 metres for women. The maximum number of gates is 10% of the drop (in metres), with a minimum of 35 in men's events and 30 in women's events.

In men's events, two jumps are permitted, one requiring a change of direction and one not. These are provided to add to the interest of the run.

Special equipment

To save vital hundredths of a second, competitors wear low-drag, one-piece clothing. The rules require them to wear crash helmets. Their skis are similar to those used in downhill events (see page 41).

Slalom and parallel slalom

In slalom events, the skier turns continuously down the course through a sequence of gates. It is a test of the skier's technical ability in performing precise, controlled, nimble turns. Speed is also important, but the turns restrict skiers to a maximum of 40kph.

Slalom course

In the Olympic and World Championship events, a slalom course should have a drop of 180-220 metres for men and 130-180 metres for women. At other international events, the drop need only be 140-220 metres and 120-180 metres respectively.

In World Championship and Olympic events the angle of the slope is also specified. It should be between 18 and 24 degrees and, for very short stretches, as much as 27 degrees.

Angle of slope
27°
18°— 24°

Within these limits, there is a wide freedom of choice in laying out the gates. The aim is to create a run which gives competitors the opportunity to combine maximum speed with maximum skill and elegance in the turns. There must be a combination of single and multiple gates, some traverses and plenty of tight turns. There should be a minimum of four hairpin gates and two combinations of closed gates, as shown on the right.

The difficulty of the course is geared to the average ability of the best 30 competitors.

The snow on the course must be even harder than in the other slalom events.

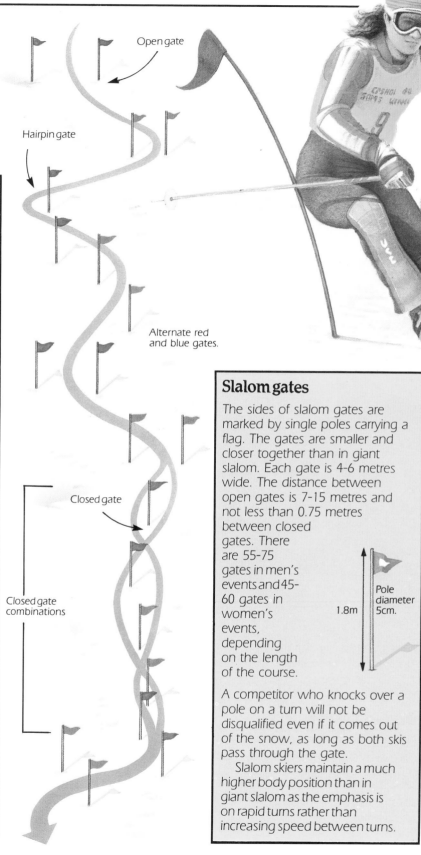

Open gate

Hairpin gate

Alternate red and blue gates.

Closed gate

Closed gate combinations

Slalom gates

The sides of slalom gates are marked by single poles carrying a flag. The gates are smaller and closer together than in giant slalom. Each gate is 4-6 metres wide. The distance between open gates is 7-15 metres and not less than 0.75 metres between closed gates. There are 55-75 gates in men's events and 45-60 gates in women's events, depending on the length of the course.

1.8m

Pole diameter 5cm.

A competitor who knocks over a pole on a turn will not be disqualified even if it comes out of the snow, as long as both skis pass through the gate.

Slalom skiers maintain a much higher body position than in giant slalom as the emphasis is on rapid turns rather than increasing speed between turns.

Slalom techniques

Slalom skiers aim to choose the "best" line through the gates, which is not necessarily the shortest route. "Good" and "bad" lines are shown on the right. The skiers aim to turn before the gate rather than after it so that they do not have to brake sharply and can make smooth, rounded turns. These are faster than short, skidded turns.

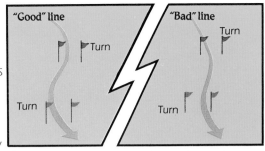

The techniques used by slalom skiers varies. Some experts succeed by taking a "bad line" because they are so fast on the turns.

Digital clock

The slalom race

The winner is the skier with the fastest combined time over two runs done on different courses. Competitors are timed electronically, as in other alpine events.

The starting order is decided in the same way as for giant slalom (see page 36).

Parallel slalom

In parallel slalom competitors race each other rather than the clock down identical courses. Each contest is based on two runs. Skiers swap courses for the second run. Electronic timing records the difference between the finishing times of the competitors in thousandths of a second. The winner is decided on the combined time differences of the two runs.

The course

The twin courses must be as nearly identical as possible. They are much shorter than for the single slalom event, with a drop of 80-100 metres and 20-30 gates. The race only lasts for about 20 to 25 seconds.

The race

The starting gates lift automatically when the starting gun is fired. A fast start is important, as the skier who is first away is often the first to finish.

If both competitors fall, the one who goes over the finish line first, wearing both skis, wins.

If one competitor fails to finish, he or she is disqualified. If both fail to finish, the one who skied furthest down the course goes through to the next round.

The competition is organized on a knockout basis, with five rounds. The winner of each goes through to the next round, as shown below. The overall winner skis 10 races in succession.

This event has not yet been accepted in the Olympics and is only occasionally allowed to contribute to World Cup points. It is very exciting to watch, so is a popular event.

Parallel slalom knockout

1st round
2nd round
3rd round
4th round
Finals

Winner

The gate poles are the same as for giant slalom.

Downhill and the flying kilometre

Downhill racing is the oldest and most spectacular alpine skiing event. Competitors ski as fast as 140km/h, in a race against the clock on courses groomed to make them as safe as possible.

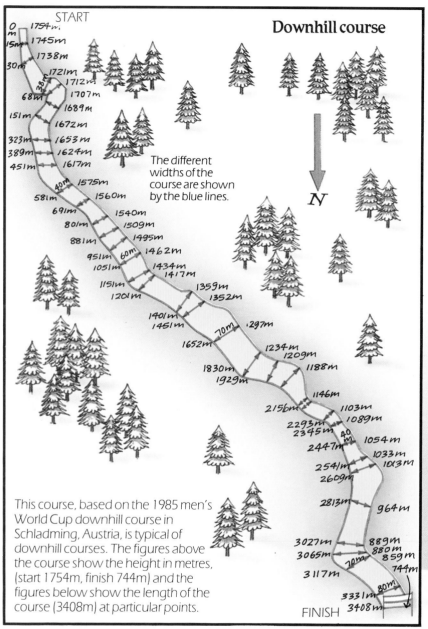

Downhill course

START
0 m 1754m
15m 1745m
30m 1738m
1721m
48m 1712m
68m 1707m
1689m
151m 1672m
323m 1653m
389m 1624m
451m 1617m
40m 1575m
581m 1560m
691m 1540m
801m 1509m
881m 1495m
951m 1462m
60m 1434m
1051m 1417m
1151m 1359m
1201m 1352m
1401m
1451m
70m 1297m
1652m 1234m
1209m
1830m 1188m
1929m
1146m
2156m 1103m
1089m
2293m
2345m 1054m
40m
2447m 1033m
1013m
2541m
2609m
2813m 964m
3027m 889m
3065m 880m
859m
70m
3117m 744m
80m
3331m
3408m
FINISH

N

The different widths of the course are shown by the blue lines.

This course, based on the 1985 men's World Cup downhill course in Schladming, Austria, is typical of downhill courses. The figures above the course show the height in metres, (start 1754m, finish 744m) and the figures below show the length of the course (3408m) at particular points.

The course

In major downhill events, the drop is 800-1000 metres for men and 500-700 metres for women. The competition is judged on one run only, but can be split into two runs of at least 450 metres each if the necessary drop cannot be achieved in one course. This is not allowed in the World and Continental Cups.

The course must be smooth and steep enough for skiers to schuss all the way without needing to use their poles.

F.I.S. regulations state that it must not be possible to complete a men's course in less than 2 minutes or a women's course in less than 1 minute 40 seconds. All obstacles, bumps and hard ridges are removed and gates are placed along the course to limit the skier's speed.

For safety reasons, the course must be at least 30 metres wide where it is bordered by trees. Where the course bends, there must be clear areas each side to limit the risk of injury if a skier goes off the course.

Twigs and pine needles are strewn on the course to help the skiers see bumps and dips. This is particularly important in poor visibility.

Training for the race

All competitors must complete strictly controlled, compulsory training on the course before the event. This takes place over three days, although in very bad weather, the time is reduced. There have to be at least three training runs and competitors are timed on at least one of them.

Starting order

The top fifteen skiers from previous results start first. Their starting order is determined by a draw. The other competitors start in order of their previous results. The first fifteen have an advantage over the others, as the course is usually at its best before too many competitors have skied it.

Downhill technique

Speed is the most important factor in ▶ downhill racing so competitors must keep their wind resistance as low as possible. This is done by adopting the "egg position" between turns, as shown to the right.

Egg position

The skier's knees and body are bent low, with his chest almost touching his knees. Special bent poles are tucked in close.

Turning

◀ To turn, as shown to the left, the skier uses a more upright stance as it is very difficult to steer in the egg position. Arms are held well forwards to help balance the body.

Throughout the course, the skiers absorb bumps with their knees while keeping the pressure of the skis constant on the snow. Some bumps make skiers take off and lose contact with the snow. This slows them down. To compensate, skiers often "pre-jump" before a bump to help stay on the snow, as shown below. ▼

Pre-jumping

She pulls her knees right up just before the bump.

The skier comes out of the egg position as she approaches the bump.

After the bump, she bends forwards and goes back into the egg position.

Downhill courses also include larger jumps. Competitors keep as low as possible as they take off, to lessen their wind resistance.

Equipment

Downhill skis are long, about 215-230cm, fairly wide and heavy. The poles are bent so that they fit around the body to help lessen wind resistance.

All racers wear one-piece lightweight suits, designed to keep down wind resistance. Crash helmets are compulsory.

The flying kilometre

The flying kilometre is a speed trial, restricted by F.I.S. regulations to men only. In a straight downhill schuss, competitors reach speeds of over 200 km/h. This event is not an official part of the skiing calendar, but there are usually 3-5 contests per year.

The course is perfectly smooth, with no turns or obstacles. After a run-in, the slope gradually increases to 45°. The skier is electronically timed over the last 100 metres of this slope.

At the end of the course, the slope gradually flattens and then goes slightly uphill over at least 300 metres. The run-out at the end of the course is often the most dangerous part, as the skier's body can be flung off balance as his skis slow down.

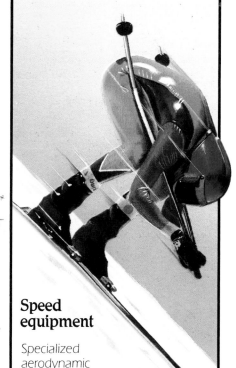

Speed equipment

Specialized aerodynamic equipment is extremely important in order to break speed records. Competitors use long skis, tight-fitting boots, aerodynamically designed crash helmets and skin-tight suits. Poles are bent, as for downhill racing.

Ski jumping

Ski jumping was originated by Sondre Norheim in Norway about 100 years ago*, and is one of the oldest competitive skiing events. Ski jumping is highly specialized and is restricted to men only. For most skiers, it is only a spectator sport. Skiers launch themselves into the air at about 100 km/h from specially built jumps - the aim being to stay in the air for as long as possible, whilst maintaining perfect control and style.

Ski jumping is held as an individual event and together with the 15 kilometre cross-country race in the Nordic combined event (see page 44).

Before the competition begins, trial jumps are made by non-competitors. These jumps, together with snow conditions and wind speed, determine how long the in-run should be so that the jumpers land on or around the table-point.

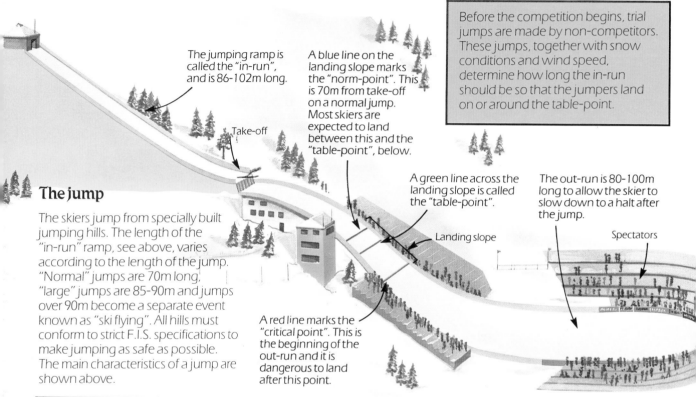

The jumping ramp is called the "in-run", and is 86-102m long.

A blue line on the landing slope marks the "norm-point". This is 70m from take-off on a normal jump. Most skiers are expected to land between this and the "table-point", below.

A green line across the landing slope is called the "table-point".

The out-run is 80-100m long to allow the skier to slow down to a halt after the jump.

Landing slope

Spectators

Take-off

A red line marks the "critical point". This is the beginning of the out-run and it is dangerous to land after this point.

The jump

The skiers jump from specially built jumping hills. The length of the "in-run" ramp, see above, varies according to the length of the jump. "Normal" jumps are 70m long, "large" jumps are 85-90m and jumps over 90m become a separate event known as "ski flying". All hills must conform to strict F.I.S. specifications to make jumping as safe as possible. The main characteristics of a jump are shown above.

Ski jumping technique

Take-off

In-run

Egg position

Stretches legs and pushes off with feet.

The skier skis down the in-run to the take-off in the "egg position", picking up as much speed as possible. No ski poles are allowed, and the skier holds his hands behind his body.

On take-off, the skier will reach speeds of up to 105 km/h. He jumps by stretching his legs sharply and pushing off with his feet to propel his body upwards and forwards over the ski tips.

In the air, his skis are parallel and fairly close. He leans over his skis and keeps his arms close to his body. To begin with, the ski tips tilt up slightly to give aerodynamic lift, like an aircraft wing.

What the judges look for

Each competitor is judged on two jumps, although they can do an optional trial jump first. The scores for the two jumps are added for the final result.

In a perfect jump, the skier keeps his skis close together, parallel and horizontal. He must not wave his arms in flight, although he can use his arms to maintain balance when landing. The F.I.S. regulations state that: "The ideal jump shall be executed with power, boldness and precision. It shall at the same time give the impression of calmness, steadiness and control".

Ski-jumping style has changed over the years. This picture shows what was considered to be "perfect style" in the 1930s, which is very different to the aerodynamic positions used by ski-jumpers today.

Scoring

Scores are awarded for style and the length of the jump, measured from take-off to landing.

Points for the length of the jump are taken from the distance beyond the norm-point.

There are five style judges. The skier begins with 20 points, losing them for faults. Faults in the in-run and out-run are not counted, although the take-off, flight and landing must be perfect for maximum points. If the skier falls or touches the snow with his hands after landing, he receives an automatic penalty of 10 points. The highest and lowest of the five style scores are discarded, so just three scores count.

Special equipment

Ski jumpers wear one-piece, lightweight, close-fitting clothing to keep the wind resistance as low as possible. The skis are much longer, wider, heavier and have more grooves underneath than normal cross-country skis, to help give lift and stability in flight. Special bindings allow the jumper to lean right forward. Helmets are worn for safety reasons.

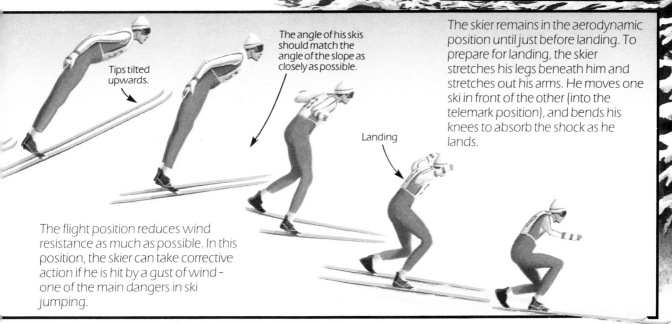

Tips tilted upwards.

The angle of his skis should match the angle of the slope as closely as possible.

Landing

The skier remains in the aerodynamic position until just before landing. To prepare for landing, the skier stretches his legs beneath him and stretches out his arms. He moves one ski in front of the other (into the telemark position), and bends his knees to absorb the shock as he lands.

The flight position reduces wind resistance as much as possible. In this position, the skier can take corrective action if he is hit by a gust of wind - one of the main dangers in ski jumping.

Cross-country racing and biathlon

The first skiing competitions were races on cross-country skis. Today, cross-country racing is split into five main events: individual racing, relay racing, the Nordic combined (jumping and racing), the biathlon (shooting and racing combined), and marathons.

All these events are held in varied, rolling countryside, with a mixture of downhill, uphill and flat sections. There are rules about the amount and length of climbs on each course. The skiers ski in tracks (see page 30), or skate on a pisted way with refreshment stations every 7-8km.

Individual racing

Competitors in this event leave the starting line at 30 second intervals for a race against the clock. The skier with the fastest time wins.

In the Olympics and World Cup, the courses are 10-50km for men, and 5-20km for women.

Techniques used

Traditional cross-country includes the diagonal stride, double pole-push, herringbone and downhill techniques. In the early 1980's traditionalists were upset by the introduction of the skating step. This is much faster than older techniques, but lacks grace and destroys the tracks*.

After much debate, the F.I.S. ruled that the skating step can be used in half of the 1986/7 and 1987/8 World

Skating step

Traditonal technique

Cup events, and in the 1988 Olympics. Traditional events will be called "classic", and others which include skating steps will be called

Overtaking

Skiers must give way to let faster skiers overtake.

"freestyle" events. The future of classic and freestyle techniques depends on how popular they are over the next few seasons.

Relay

Relay racing rules are the same as for individual racing, but with a few additions. The skiers compete in teams of four and each person skis on one leg of the course. There are four 10km legs in men's events and four 5km legs in women's events.

The first skiers in each team start together. After the first 100 metres, the starting tracks converge to form three tracks. At the end of each leg there is a 30m change over area where the skiers hand-over by touching the next skier in their team.

Equipment

Cross-country racers use skis specialized for either the classic-style or the skating step. Classic skiers may occasionally need to stop and rewax their skis on long races. Competitors may replace both poles during the race, but only one ski, making the change without assistance. They wear lightweight, one-piece clothing.

Nordic combined

The Nordic combined is regarded by many as the elite Nordic event, but it is still confined to men only. The competition takes place over three days. Normally on the first two days each competitor does three jumps from a 70km hill, of which the best two count. On the third day they enter a 15km cross-country race. The winner is determined by the combined results.

* Traditional cross-country techniques and the skating step are described on pages 30-31.

Biathlon

The biathlon combines cross-country racing with target shooting, having its origins in the use of skis for military purposes and hunting. Most competitors in this specialized event train in their armed forces. This is the only event not governed by the F.I.S., but by a body called the Union International de Pentathlon Moderne et Biathlon.

There are three main events in the World Cup and Olympics, outlined below.

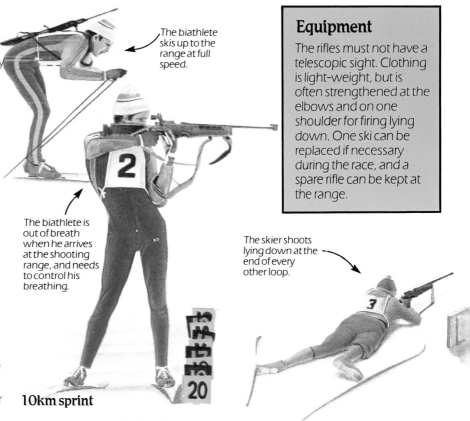

The biathlete skis up to the range at full speed.

The biathlete is out of breath when he arrives at the shooting range, and needs to control his breathing.

The skier shoots lying down at the end of every other loop.

Equipment

The rifles must not have a telescopic sight. Clothing is light-weight, but is often strengthened at the elbows and on one shoulder for firing lying down. One ski can be replaced if necessary during the race, and a spare rifle can be kept at the range.

20km race

The course has five 4km cross-country loops which are arranged around a central point where the starting line, finishing line and rifle ranges are set. The course itself must have height differences of 550-750m.

The skiers carry 4.5kg rifles on their back and 20 rounds of ammunition. At the end of all except the last loop, the skiers enter the firing range and fire five rounds at targets 50m away. A one minute penalty is added to a competitor's overall time for each target left standing. An average time for completing such a course is one hour.

10km sprint

The 10km sprint is divided into three loops with a height distance over the course of 300-400m. There are two firing sessions, one lying down and the other standing. In this event, for each target missed the competitor skis a penalty loop of 150 metres, which takes about 30 seconds to do.

30km relay

There are four biathletes in each relay team. Each member skis 7.5km with two firing sessions, one lying down and the other standing. As with cross-country relay, there is a mass start by all the first skiers.

Marathons

Ski marathons, called "citizen racing" in America, are long distance races (from 40-150km) which anyone can enter. They are very popular and can attract mass starts of over 10,000 skiers of all ages and abilities. Some marathons, such as the Canadian ski marathon, are two day events in which advanced competitors camp out overnight.

Ten of the world's major marathons have grouped together to form Worldloppet, an international ski series. Anyone who competes in all of them in the course of their life receives a special medal.

The first ski marathons follow routes taken in famous historical events. You can find out more about these on page 55.

Aerials and moguls

There are three kinds of freestyle skiing, called aerials, mogul skiing and ballet. Aerials and mogul skiing are explained here; freestyle ballet and its techniques on pages 48-49.

History of freestyle

Freestyle is new to competitive skiing, and will be introduced as a demonstration sport for the first time at the 1988 Olympic Games in Calgary, Canada.

Freestyle developed in America in the late sixties/seventies as an attempt to break away from strictly stylized skiing, such as "perfect" parallel turns, and to add more freedom, fun and challenge to skiing. Most skiing competitions began on an amateur basis, but freestyle competition started as a professional sport. The attraction of prize money and the lack of set rules, led competitors to take many risks. In 1973, following some serious accidents, the freestyle skiers organized themselves into a professional body to control safety and draw up competition rules. In 1979, freestyle was accepted into the F.I.S., the organization which governs all skiing competitions, and freestyle gained the credibility it had previously lacked.

Aerials

Aerials are the most exciting of the three freestyle disciplines. They can also be very dangerous, and the rules drawn up by the F.I.S. are particularly strict.

The three main types of aerial manoeuvres are jumps called uprights, front somersaults and back somersaults. The easiest jumps are uprights, such as the side twist. The helicopter is also an upright jump but it is slightly more complicated as it involves a 360° spin.

Side twist

Helicopter

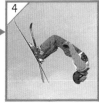

Somersault

Somersaults are the most difficult and spectacular aerials. The photographs above show a layout back somersault.

Safety

No jumps should be attempted without qualified instruction. Training begins on trampolines which help to increase body awareness in flight. The pupil then practises on artificial jumps into water. Once the aerial manoeuvre and landing has been perfected in this way, the pupil can attempt aerials on snow. All aerial competitors need to present a certificate of competence from a qualified judge or an experienced jumper.

Take off

In all aerial competitions, the skier takes off from a specially built jump, called a kicker. There are usually three different heights of kickers depending on whether a single, double or triple somersault is being performed. The highest, most steeply curved kicker is used for triple somersaults. Upright jumps, as well as single somersaults, are performed from the smallest kicker.

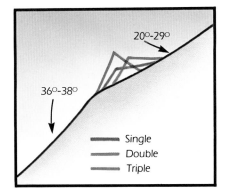

The run in slope to the kickers is at an angle of 20° to 29°. The landing slope needs to be within the angles of 36° to 38° to prevent hard impact on landing. The landing slope itself is continually softened with a shovel to ease landing.

What the judges look for

In the past, jumps were judged according to how visually exciting they were. Now, in the interest of safety, the emphasis is on perfection. Before each jump, the competitor informs the jury of the figure he is to perform.

Scores are awarded in the following manner:

* Technical performance (out of 5)
* Height and distance (out of 2)
* Extent of jump & landing (out of 3)

Complex jumps performed well are worth more than simple jumps. The judges multiply the score for each jump by a factor based on the degree of difficulty of the jump to reach a final score.

Mogul skiing

In mogul skiing, competitors ski a mogul slope* to loud music, jumping and turning as often as possible. The skier is limited to upright aerials only.

The course is approximately 250 metres long, with a steep (28° to 35°) and heavily moguled incline. The competitors start through a gate which triggers the electronic timing.

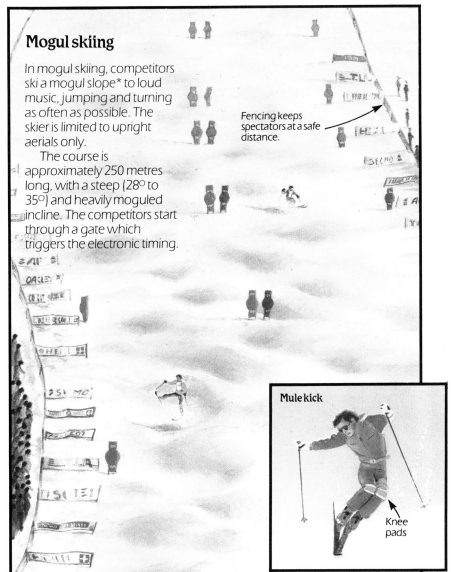

Fencing keeps spectators at a safe distance.

Mule kick

Knee pads

There is a smooth, clear area at the bottom of the course where skiers come to a controlled stop. The judges stand below this, where they can see the whole slope.

Jumps, such as the "mule kick" above, are scored highly in mogul skiing. Landing is difficult on a steep mogul slope, and the skier must time the jump perfectly in order not to break the continuity of the run. The skier wears bright knee pads to heighten his movements.

What the judges look for

Scores are awarded in the following manner:

* Technique, i.e. ease of action on a very uneven course (out of 5)
* The two best jumps (out of 2.5)
* Electronically timed speed (out of 2.5).

At the beginning of the competition, a finalist from a previous competition skis the course and acts as a pace setter for speed. The speed points for each competitor are set against this.

The top 8 go through to the finals, which are held in pairs - two finalists compete side by side down the course.

*See pages 18-19.

Ballet and simple ballet technique

Freestyle ballet is a mixture of figure skating and gymnastics performed on snow. The skier "dances" to music broadcast over a smooth 250m course, sloping at 11° to 16°. The snow should be dry, well packed and easy to ski on.

Ballet technique

Freestyle ballet can be done by any competent skier. The only limits are your level of fitness and imagination. For ballet skiing you need a good sense of balance and the ability to shift your weight freely from one ski to another. The techniques shown here will help you develop these skills and improve your normal alpine skiing, as well as giving you the freedom and fun of trying something new.

Boots light and flexible.

Skis short and light.

Long poles for extra leverage.

Royal Christie

The Royal Christie is said to be named after a German ice skater, Fritz Reuel (pronounced royal), who wrote the first book on ballet skiing in 1929*. A Royal Christie is a turn made on the inside ski with the outside ski raised backwards as high as possible.

Begin in the traverse position with your weight on the lower ski.

Plant your inside pole and start lifting the upper ski slightly to the side and behind.

Uphill crossover

The uphill crossover is also known as a stepover. You need to be supple for this manoeuvre, so do some leg stretching exercises before you try it to warm up your leg muscles. You can find out about exercises on pages 56-59.

Start by skiing across the fall line with your left leg slightly back and to the side.

Rock your left ski back and then kick it high up in front of you, crossing it over the right ski.

Judging

Scores are awarded out of 10 like this:

* Choreography (the ballet sequence) and originality (out of 2.5)
* Difficulty of the manoeuvres (out of 2.5)
* Technical achievement and overall impression (out of 5)

Technical achievement points are given for the degree of perfection of the figures, independently of how difficult they are.

360° spin

The 360° spin is a basic manoeuvre used a lot in freestyle ballet. Once you have mastered the basic spin shown to the right, with practice you will be able to spin round two or three times in the same way.

Start by skiing across the hill with your arms out to your sides in a ballet position.

Plant your upper pole, and bend your knees up into the hill to begin the turn.

*Fritz Reuel: New Possibilities in Skiing.

The outrigger

The outrigger is a simple freestyle manoeuvre which can be used to link up more difficult manoeuvres or when coming out of a turn. It is basically a traverse done in a low position, with the lower leg stretched out below the upper leg, as shown to the right.

Begin by traversing across the hill.

Weight on upper ski.

Bend down and stretch your lower ski out to the side.

No weight here.

Continue traversing in this low position.

Bend forward at the waist and arch your back. Begin turning by shifting weight onto the front of the ski.

With your ski flat on the snow, lean your head and shoulders into the turn. The ski will follow round.

Decrease the pressure on the front of the ski, so that the tail of the ski slips down.

Bring the lifted ski down next to the new upper ski, and return to the traverse position.

Put your left ski down about 30cm from the right ski, and shift your weight onto it.

Using your poles for balance, bend forwards at your waist and lift your right ski up behind you.

Straighten up your body and bring the right ski round parallel to the left ski.

Complete the crossover by putting down the right ski, and ski on in a ballet stance.

You will now be half way through the spin, facing directly up the hill. Keep your weight forwards.

Lean back onto the tails of your skis so that the tips swing round for the second half of the spin.

With your weight on the front of your skis push your knees forwards into the rest of the spin.

The 360° spin is now complete and you should be facing in the same direction as you started.

Pistes

All skiing resorts have specially prepared and graded runs, called pistes. Pistes are maintained and patrolled by resort authorities or ski lift companies, who make sure that the runs are safe and clearly marked according to their degree of difficulty.

Piste maintenance

The snow on pisted runs is packed into a smooth surface by machines, which also break up ruts and bumps. Mogul slopes, as described on page 18, occur on runs which are too steep for the piste machines.

Piste machine

After heavy snow fall, there may be danger of avalanches. The piste service may close runs while they blast slopes with explosives to start controlled avalanches. The pistes are re-opened when the snow has been cleared.

At the end of each day, the ski patrol ski down all the runs to check that no one is left on the mountain. The piste patrol is also responsible for bringing down injured skiers*.

How pistes are graded

Most pistes have colour-coded markers alongside according to the degree of difficulty of the run. The colour system used varies slightly from country to country.

In Europe, pistes normally fall into the four categories shown above right. Green runs are very gentle, blue runs slope up to 25%, red runs slope between 25 and 40% and black runs are usually 40% or steeper.

Piste map

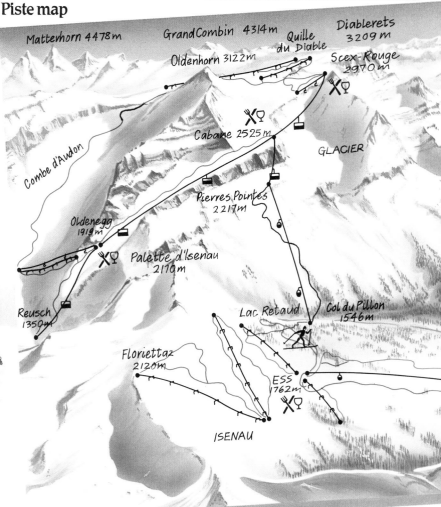

European piste codes:

Very easy beginner's run | Easy piste | Intermediate piste | Difficult piste

In the United States the coding system is as follows:

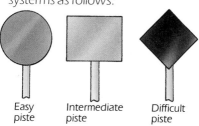

Easy piste | Intermediate piste | Difficult piste

Warning signs

Most resorts also use a system of signposts to warn of possible dangers, such as avalanches, and to inform you if a particular piste is closed. Read these carefully - NEVER ski down closed pistes.

 Danger
 Avalanche danger - piste closed
Ski lift crossing

 SOS telephone
 First aid post
 Piste closed

*See page 52 for details on accident procedure.

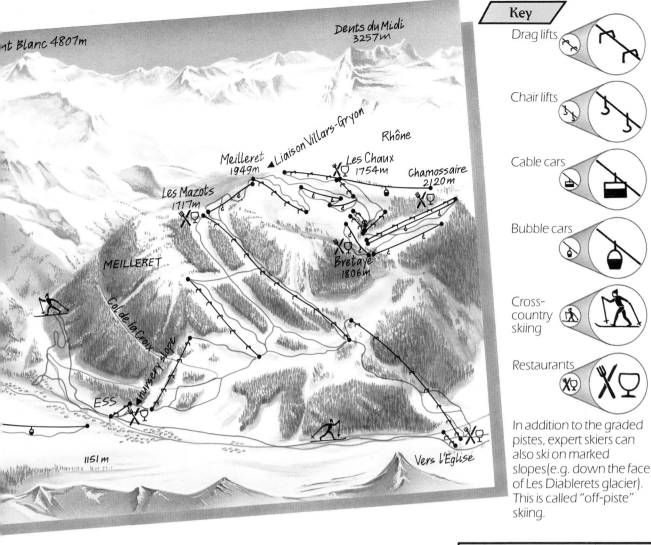

Key

Drag lifts

Chair lifts

Cable cars

Bubble cars

Cross-country skiing

Restaurants

In addition to the graded pistes, expert skiers can also ski on marked slopes (e.g. down the face of Les Diablerets glacier). This is called "off-piste" skiing.

Map labels: Mont Blanc 4807m, Dents du Midi 3257m, Meilleret 1949m, Liaison Villars-Gryon, Rhône, Les Chaux 1754m, Chamossaire 2120m, Les Mazots 1717m, Bretaye 1806m, MEILLERET, Col de la Croix, nursery slope, ESS, 1151 m, Vers l'Eglise

Piste maps

All resorts provide piste maps which show you the layout of the runs and lift systems in a resort. The piste map above is from Les Diablerets in Switzerland.

The runs are shown by colour-coded lines which correspond to their difficulty - black for difficult runs, red for intermediate runs and so on.

The lifts are shown by black lines with little symbols to show whether they are chair lifts, drag lifts, cable cars or bubble cars.

Use piste maps to plan your skiing. Always check at the lift stations what time the last lift departs so you do not find yourself stranded on the wrong side of a valley.

Tips on choosing a resort

Piste maps are available from tourist offices or from ski clubs and are probably the best guides you can get on the skiing facilities offered by a particular resort.

* The altitude of the resort is important, particularly if you are going to ski in spring.

* The greater the height distance is between the top and bottom slopes, the longer the runs will be.

* Check to see which way the slopes are facing, as this affects the snow conditions at different times of the year (see page 53).

* Check that the resort has several runs at the correct level of ability for you - if you are a beginner, choose a resort with nursery slopes and plenty of blue and green runs.

* The piste map will show whether there are cross-country tracks if you prefer to go cross-country skiing for part, or all, of your trip.

* Look out for potential bottlenecks at lifts on the piste map. If there are several runs converging on one lift system, there may be long queues for the lift.

Safety and snow conditions

Although skiing accidents occur, many can be avoided by being aware of the limits of your own ability and by skiing sensibly with consideration for others. Keep in mind the safety points below.

Safety points to remember

* Always ski with others in mind. Choose a route down the slope so as not to endanger the skier in front. When you overtake, leave them plenty of room to manoeuvre - the skier in front always has the right of way.

Overtaking

* Keep in control. Adapt your speed and movements to your own level of ability and to the weather, terrain and snow conditions.

* Do not ski alone in poor visibility. Ski on runs you know, and keep within sight of the piste markers. In fog and blizzards, do not go out. If you are already skiing, head for a safe place, such as a lift station.

Blizzard

* If you are about to join or traverse across a piste, check first that your route is free of skiers.

* Do not stop (except in emergencies) in the middle of the piste, or on a bend where you cannot be seen by following skiers. If you fall, move out of the way as quickly as you can.

Do not obstruct the piste.

* Take notice of piste markers and warning signs, and instructions from the piste patrol.

* Keep to the edge of the piste if you climb up it and if you walk down without skis.

* Learn how to fall correctly (see page 7) to avoid hurting yourself.

* If you see an accident, stop and help if you can. Do not try to move the injured skier. If possible, one person should remain to comfort the person and warn oncoming skiers of the accident, whilst another goes for help. Ski to the bottom of the nearest lift to contact the rescue service. Make sure you know the precise location of the accident (from the nearest piste marker or lift pylon, which are usually numbered).

Mountain rescue

* Never ski off-piste on your own. If you are inexperienced, go with a guide or ski teacher. Off-piste runs are not patrolled, and you ski them at your own risk. Check with the piste patrol about possible avalanches before you go and learn to judge avalanche risk for yourself (for instance, don't ski down overhanging slopes after a heavy snow fall).

Avalanches are most likely on exposed slopes of between 30° and 45°. New snowfall increases the risk, as does wind - it can build up drifts. A sudden rise of temperature may trigger off an avalanche, particularly in spring.

* It is a good idea to protect yourself with a comprehensive winter sports insurance - medical treatment and transport from the mountain, possibly by helicopter, can be very expensive.

Snow conditions

The things that affect snow conditions most are the time of year, the altitude of the slopes, the direction slopes face, and the amount of wind.

Altitude

Temperature falls the higher up you go - on average, there is a 1° drop in temperature for every 100m. Because of this the skiing season is longer in high areas, as snow falls first on high slopes, and takes longer to melt than on lower slopes.

In the northern hemisphere, the skiing season lasts from about December to the middle of April, and in the southern hemisphere, from June to October. There are also areas where you can ski on glaciers all year round. The snow conditions change throughout the season as the air temperature increases.

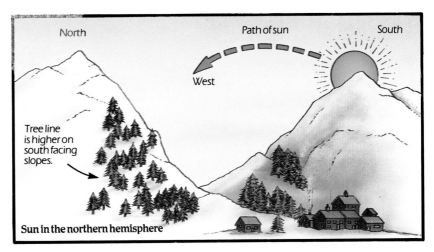

Tree line is higher on south facing slopes.

Sun in the northern hemisphere

Slope direction

The direction the slopes face affects the amount of sun they get, which in turn affects the snow conditions. In the northern hemisphere, south-facing slopes receive more sun than north-facing slopes and vice versa in the southern hemisphere.

In mid-winter, the sun is not very strong, so it has little effect on the snow conditions. It is usually more pleasant to ski on sunny slopes as it is very cold in the shade.

In the last two months of the skiing season the snow on sunny slopes can become wet and soupy (see below) so snow conditions will be better on shady slopes.

Chart of snow conditions

The following chart describes some different snow conditions you may come across, their causes, and tips on how to ski in them.

Type of snow	How to recognize it	Cause	Skiing tips
Powder	Fine, light ice crystals - will not make snowballs.	New snow in calm, dry, cold conditions.	Excellent for skiing on-piste and perfect off-piste conditions.
Soup	Wet, sticky snow - makes good snowballs.	Warm conditions.	Very slow conditions. Wax skis and ski as close to the fall line as possible - be ready for sudden acceleration if you hit fast snow.
Crust	Hard, crusted surface.	Snow has melted and refrozen, or is windblown.	Make yourself as light as possible. Keep your weight balanced equally over both skis and keep them flat on the snow.
Ice	Solid, hard and smooth.	Repeated melting and refreezing of the snow.	Keep your skis well edged with extra weight on the lower ski. Ski as close as possible to the edge of the piste, where it is usually less icy.

The history of skiing

Skis have been used for centuries by Lapps, Finns and Scandinavians for hunting across frozen country. It is only in the last century that skiing has spread to the rest of the world and developed as a pleasure sport.

Prehistoric skis

Prehistoric skis have been found in Sweden, Norway and Finland. The oldest ski found was at Hoting, in Sweden, and is about 4500 years old. The Hoting ski is made of pine and is 111cm long. A foot piece has been scooped out of the wood and there are holes through which basic bindings could have been fitted, as shown below.

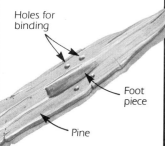

Holes for binding

Foot piece

Pine

Rock carvings of skiers have been found in Russia and Norway. The oldest, which is the same age as the Hoting ski, was found at Rödöy, a Norwegian Island just north of the Arctic Circle. This carving appears to be of a man hunting - he is wearing a headdress with hare-like ears and is carrying a hooked pole which may have been a hunting weapon.

Skiing myths and legends

Little is known about the early history of skiing, but there are some interesting myths; and some legends which may be based on fact.

The legend of King Håkon

King Håkon ruled Norway from 1217 to 1263. When he was two years old his life was threatened by rivals to his father's throne.

Two loyal skiers rescued the child and carried him to safety across the Dovre mountains during a snowstorm.

The Birkebeiner cross-country race follows the route of the Norwegians who rescued King Håkon. The race is named after the birch-bark leggings they wore.

Gustav Vasa's war of liberation

In 1520 the Danes defeated the Swedes and executed 82 of their leaders in Stockholm. Gustav Vasa, one of the remaining leaders, tried to rally the Swedes at a town called Mora for a war of liberation. They refused to help him and he was forced to flee on snow-shoes towards the Norwegian border. The people changed their minds and sent their two best skiers to bring Vasa back to lead the Swedes to freedom. The skiers caught up with him at Sälen and he returned with them

Norse mythology

Ancient Scandinavian myths include tales of Skadi, a giantess who loved skiing and hunting.

Skadi's father, the giant Thiazi, was killed by the gods in a feud. To end the feud the gods tried to appease the furious Skadi with gold. Instead of gold, Skadi asked for a husband, hoping to marry Balder, the fairest, most gentle and wise of gods. The gods agreed, but she had to make her choice of husband by his feet only. The beautiful, white feet she chose did not belong to Balder, but to Njord, god of the sea.

At first they agreed to split their time between the mountains and the sea, spending nine months in each. Skadi hated the sea and Njord hated the mountains. In the end, Skadi returned to the mountains where she hunted on skis with a bow.

to Mora, where he defeated the Danes and became King of Sweden in 1523.

In 1922 the Vasa cross-country race was founded to celebrate the 400th anniversary of this event. The race goes from Sälen to Mora, 85.8km, and has annual entries of over 10,000 competitors.

The spread of skiing

One of the mysteries of skiing history is the lack of evidence of skiing south of Norway, Sweden and northern Russia until the 19th century, with one exception. In 1689 a book written by Johann Valvasor describes peasants in parts of Yugoslavia skiing down the mountains. They had skis with leather strap bindings and a large pole to lean back on and steer with.

There is no evidence of skiing in the Alps until nearly 200 years later. One reason for this may be that Alp communities came down into the valleys during the winter to relatively mild, snowless climates - an option not available to the people of the far North.

Gold rush skiing

In the mid-19th century, skiing was spread by Scandinavian immigrants to the gold rush areas of North America and Australia. The world's first ski club, called the Kiandra Club, was founded in 1861 by a Norwegian in the Snowy Mountains in Australia.

◀ In California, a Norwegian immigrant called John Thompson, offered to carry the mail 500km across the Sierra Nevada on skis. He began in 1856 and continued to carry mail backwards and forwards along the same route for 20 years.

Recent history

Skiing as known today began to develop as a sport in Norway. Much of its progress was due to a few pioneers, described below.

Sondre Norheim

The Norwegian, Sondre Norheim is often called the father of competitive skiing. In about 1840, he was the first person to jump on skis off hillsides, 30 metres down onto steep slopes. Before Norheim, people had only jumped onto flat or slightly sloping land.

Norheim also developed skiing equipment. First he made bindings with a heel strap which gave more control over his skis. He then changed the shape of skis by giving them a curved waist, which is still a major part of ski design today.

With his advanced equipment, Norheim was able to develop controlled turns, such as the telemark* (named after his home town) and win many Norwegian competitions.

* See page 33.

Fridtjof Nansen

In 1888 Fridtjof Nansen led a Norwegian expedition across Greenland on skis. He wrote a best-selling book about the trip, with tips on cross-country, hunting and jumping techniques. This spread enthusiasm for skiing throughout Europe but it did not explain how to ski on steep alpine slopes.

Mathias Zdarsky

Mathias Zdarsky, an Austrian, read Nansens's book and was "seized with the Nansen fever". He bought a pair of skis 294cm long with cane bindings and no toe piece to stop the heel moving sideways on the ski. He had a long, single pole to help him steer.

Zdarsky had no control on steep slopes with his skis. He shortened them to 220cm and, after many experiments, made a binding with a rigid metal toe piece so that his heel could not move sideways (although it still lifted up and down). Then, through trial and error he discovered the stem turn, and was able to control his descents.

Zdarsky wrote a book about alpine techniques, which attracted lots of people to come to him for skiing lessons. Alpine skiing, as known today, had begun.

After Zdarsky, alpine techniques and equipment evolved quickly as its popularity increased. Only 50 years ago skis were still made from wood, and leather boots were attached to them by strap bindings - very different to the sophisticated equipment of today**.

** See page 34 for the history of competition skiing.

55

Pre-skiing exercises

Skiing requires stamina, flexibility and strength. The fitter you are before going skiing, the more you will enjoy yourself. If you are not very fit, you will tire easily, you may strain muscles that you do not normally use and you will spend a lot of your holiday stiff and aching.

Younger people tend to be naturally more supple than older people, so as a general rule you will not need to do any specific pre-skiing exercises if you are under the age of about 15. If you want to build up the level of your fitness, do plenty of swimming, bicycling and sports you enjoy.

There are some specific exercises, given on the next four pages, which help prepare various parts of the body for skiing. Start exercising about two months before going skiing and do each exercise 3-5 times a week. Always begin with a 15 minute warm-up, as described on the opposite page, so that you do not strain your muscles.

Never push yourself beyond your own level of fitness. Gradually build up the number of exercises you do and stop immediately if any exercise hurts. In addition to these exercises, walk whenever possible, swim, bicycle and keep generally fit.

Muscles used in skiing

This diagram shows the muscles and parts of the body which are used most in skiing.

Shoulders and arms

Your shoulders and arms need to be strong for pole-planting, for pushing yourself along on your poles on the flat and for climbing uphill.

Stomach and back

Stomach and back muscles need to be strong and supple in order for you to balance well.

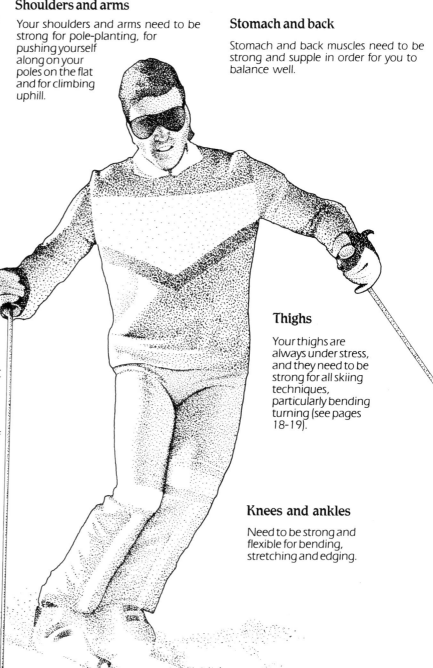

Thighs

Your thighs are always under stress, and they need to be strong for all skiing techniques, particularly bending turning (see pages 18-19).

Knees and ankles

Need to be strong and flexible for bending, stretching and edging.

General stamina

You need stamina for all skiing and particularly for cross-country skiing where you need to climb and push yourself along on the flat as often as skiing downhill.

Warm-up exercises

 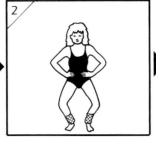  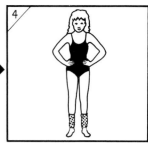

Exercise 1: Stand on your toes, legs slightly apart,

hands on your hips. Bend your knees until you sit on

your heels. Keep your back straight. Then, keeping on

your toes, stretch up as high as you can. Repeat 15 times.

Exercise 2: With your hands on your hips, feet slightly apart and flat on the

ground, rotate your hips around in a circle. Do this 10

times in a clockwise direction and then 10 times

in an anticlockwise direction.

  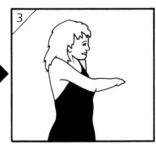 

Exercise 3: Stand with your legs apart and feet flat on the ground. Hold one arm bent

across your chest and swing your other arm to the side and behind you. Then do

the same on the other side. Do not strain yourself. Do 10 swings to each side.

Exercise 4: Jog on the spot for five minutes.

Skiing exercises

The following exercises will strengthen the muscles you use when skiing and will make them more supple.

Getting up from a fall

Try this exercise, particularly if you are a beginner skier, which is good practice for getting up again after a fall*.

 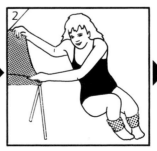 

Sit on the floor beside a chair. Hold the chair back with your inside hand and the seat with your other

hand. With your feet parallel and fairly close together, stand up by pushing with your legs and pressing

against the chair with your arms. Sit down again. Do the exercise 6 times on each side.

* See page 7.

Shoulders and arms

  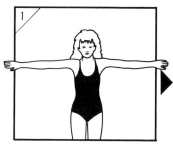 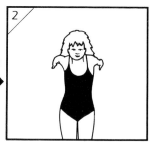

Exercise 1: Stand and shrug both your shoulders together 10 times. Then

shrug alternate shoulders 20 times. This will loosen up your shoulder muscles.

Exercise 2: Stand with your arms out sideways, palms facing back. Press your arms back as far as you can. Hold

for a few seconds. Repeat 10 times. This will strengthen your shoulder muscles.

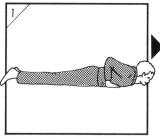  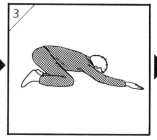 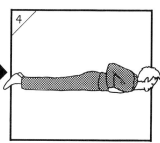

Exercise 3: Lie face down on the floor, with your hands flat on the floor next

to your shoulders. Push up on your arms, keeping your knees and toes on the floor.

Then sink back onto your heels and stretch your arms out in front of you. Repeat

this 15 times. This exercise strengthens both your shoulders and arms.

Back muscles

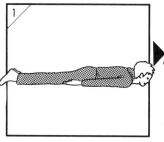 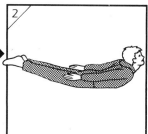

Stomach and thigh muscles

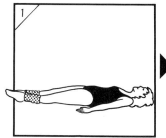 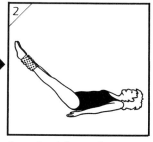

Lie on your front, with your arms by your sides. At the same time, lift your chest

and legs as far as you can. Repeat 10-15 times.

Lie on your back, arms by your sides. Slowly lift both your legs until they are at right angles to the floor,

then slowly lower them. Repeat 10-15 times. This strengthens your stomach and thigh muscles.

Stomach muscles

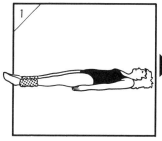   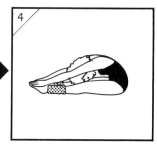

Lie on your back, with your arms by your sides. Raise yourself up, taking the strain

on your stomach muscles, and bend right forwards to touch your toes. If you find

this very difficult, wedge your feet under a chair or sofa. Repeat 10-15 times.

This will strengthen your stomach muscles.

Thigh muscles

 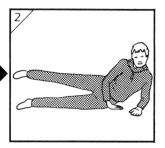  

Exercise 1: Lie on your side, legs parallel, arms in front for balance. Lift your top leg up about 30cm and hold it

there for a few seconds. Do this 10 times and then repeat on the other side.

Exercise 2: Stand with your legs apart, one knee bent and the other stretched out straight, hands on your hips. Keep your knee over the big toe of your bent leg. This leg takes most of your weight. Keep your hips low and transfer your weight onto the other leg, by bending your straight leg and stretching your bent leg.

Shift from side to side 20 times, and then do it more

slowly, holding the position to each side whilst you count to ten.

Exercise 3: Sit unsupported against a wall with your feet flat on the ground, thighs parallel to the floor and your lower legs bent at 90°. Hold this position for 30 seconds to begin with. Each day you do the exercise build up the time until you can hold it for up to two minutes. This is one of the most important skiing exercises as it greatly strengthens your legs.

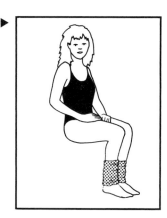

Knees and ankles

Stand with your feet next to each other and about 15cm apart. Bend down, keeping your knees above your feet.

Lower your bottom as close to your heels as possible without lifting your heels.

Leg stretching

 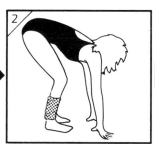  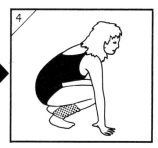

Crouch on your toes with your hands on the floor in

front of your body. Bounce your bottom up and down

three times and then stretch your legs out straight,

keeping your hands on the ground.

Legs and ankles

Stand with your feet together and jump from side to side, keeping your upper

body as still as possible. Your feet should be doing most of the work. Try to keep

jumping for a minute and build up to more jumps each time you do it. This exercise

will help you to edge your skis.

The shape of skis

As soon as you start skiing, you will find that you spend most of the time trying to control your speed down the slope. To do this you have to turn continually. This page explains how the shape of skis helps you turn.

How the side-cut helps

If you look at a ski from above, you will see that it is not the same width all the way down. Skis curve in towards the middle, making a waist near the bindings. This is called the "side-cut". Skis are also wider at the front (shovel) than at the back (tail).

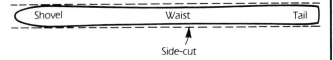

The ski's side-cut affects its turning ability: the more pronounced the side-cut, the more the shovel of the ski will bite into the snow when the ski is tilted on its edge*, and the more easily the ski will turn. The diagram below shows how this works.

1

Ski is edged in order to turn.

The wider shovel digs into the snow more than any other part of the ski.

Ski edged.

2

When you press against the edged ski, there is more resistance at the shovel than the rest of the ski, which pivots around the shovel.

Pressure against edged ski.

Shovel bites into snow.

Tail skids sideways.

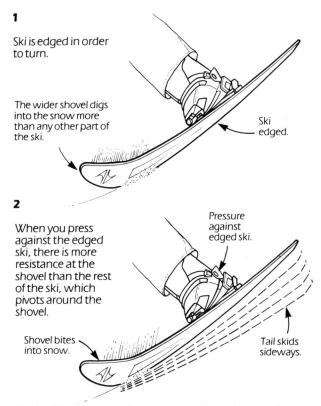

If skis did not have a side-cut, the whole ski would tend to skid sideways when you push against the edged ski, and you would not be able to steer the turn.

How the camber helps

If you look at a ski side on, you will notice that the thickness of the ski varies too. It is thicker at the centre than at the tip and tail. It also has a curved shape. When you lay a ski on a flat surface, the centre of the unweighted ski bows up. This is called the "camber".

Unweighted ski

Tail

Tip

Camber

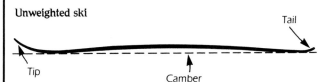

The purpose of the camber and the varying thickness of the ski is to distribute the skier's weight along the length of the ski. Without a camber your weight would be concentrated below your feet so that when you edged, only the middle of the ski would bite the snow and the ski would not turn properly.

Weighted ski

Weight evenly spread.

The camber in fast turns

When you turn at high speeds, the pressure of your legs against the edged ski is much stronger than in a normal turn. This pressure alters the camber so that, instead of bowing up, the ski bows down in the middle. This is called a "reverse camber".

On a fast turn, the reverse camber is of special importance. When the skis are edged, the bend in the ski makes the edge along the whole length of the ski bite into the snow. (In a normal turn most of the grip is at the front of the ski.) This means that the turn is fast, since the shovel is not acting as a brake, and there is minimum skidding. The ski turns in a smooth arc which is fast and fluent.

Reverse camber

Pressure from the leg makes the ski go into a reverse camber.

The edge of the ski along its whole length lies flat on the snow in a curve.

With continued pressure, the ski turns in a smooth arc, with very little skidding.

The greater the reverse camber, i.e. the stronger the leg pressure, the tighter the curve will be.

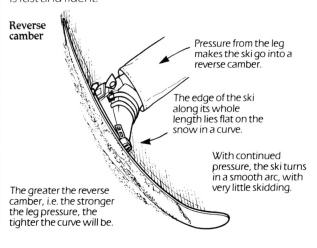

Glossary

Alpine skiing. The term used to distinguish downhill from cross-country (nordic) skiing.

Banking. Leaning your body into a turn.

Basket. A plastic disk above the tip of a ski pole which stops the pole from sinking too far into the snow.

Bending turning. A parallel turn made by bending your knees and relaxing your leg muscles to unweight your skis (called down-unweighting), before banking your knees into the turn.

Biathlon. A nordic competition which combines cross-country racing with target shooting.

Bindings. The device which attaches the bottom of a ski boot to the ski.

Blood wagon. The nickname for the sledge used to bring injured skiers downhill.

Canting. A method for adjusting your boots if you are slightly knock-kneed or bow-legged so that you stand flat on your skis.

Camber. The arch in a ski which ensures that the skier's weight is spread along the whole length of the ski, rather than remaining in the middle.

Carved turn. Turns made when the whole edge of the ski passes through a single groove in the snow.

Cornice. An overhanging ridge of snow.

Crust. Snow that has melted and refrozen, or is windblown, and has a hard, crusted surface.

Double-pole push. A technique used on fairly flat terrain to go forwards. Both poles are planted in front of your body and used to push off from whilst sliding your skis forwards.

Downhill turn. A turn made into and out of the fall line, going downhill (i.e. increasing the angle of descent).

Downhill. The fastest alpine competition event (apart from the flying kilometre). It is a timed speed contest on a specially prepared course with gates to control the skiers' speed.

Edges. The metal strips running along each side of a ski. They protect skis from wear and grip the snow when pressure is put on them.

Edging. Tilting onto the metal edges running along the sides of skis. This is done by applying more pressure to one side of the ski than the other.

Edge change. Transfer of pressure from the edges of one side of the skis to the other.

Egg position. The low crouched position used to accelerate in a schuss. Also called a "tuck".

Fall line. The steepest, shortest and fastest line down a slope.

Flying kilometre. A downhill speed trial done in a schuss. The competitor's speed is timed as he passes through a 100m section of the course.

Forerunners. Non-competitors who ski down slalom and downhill courses to check the conditions and mark a course through the gates before the race.

Freestyle. Acrobatic skiing which includes aerials, mogul skiing and ballet.

Gaiters. Waterproof cuffs worn around the bottom of ski trousers and the top of ski boots.

Gate. A set of two flags or poles through which slalom or downhill racers must ski on their way down the course. Gates can be "open" (lying across the fall line), or "closed" (lying down the fall line). Gates are alternately red and blue.

Glide zone. The front and back sections on the base of cross-country skis. Glide zones allow the ski to glide forwards when standing with equal weight on both skis.

Grip zone. The central section on the base of cross-country skis. This allows the ski to grip the snow when most of the weight is on one ski.

Grass skiing. Skiing on grass slopes with special caterpillar-track skis.

Herringbone. A method of climbing uphill with the tails of the skis together, tips apart and poles held behind for support. The skis are stepped up and edged into the slope one after the other.

Hot dog skiing. An early name for freestyle skiing.

Inner boot. Soft, removable lining which fits inside the rigid outer shell of alpine ski boots.

Inside ski. Term used for the ski inside the curve made when turning. Inside hip and pole are also defined in this way.

Kicker. Specially built jumps used for taking off in aerial manoeuvres.

Kick turn. A method for turning from stationary through 180°. One ski is lifted into a vertical position and pivoted around its tail to face the opposite way. The other ski is then lifted round parallel to the first ski.

Klister. A soft wax applied to the grip zone of cross-country skis. It helps the ski grip the snow and stops it sliding backwards.

Lower ski. Term used for the lower of the two skis when you are skiing across the fall line.

Marathon. A long distance cross-country race which anyone can enter. Called "citizen racing" in America.

Mogul. A bump on the piste, often formed by a succession of skiers turning at the same point.

Mogul field. A slope covered in bumps. Found on slopes too steep to be beaten down by piste machines.

Mono-skiing. Skiing done on one, wide ski.

Nordic. Cross-country skiing. It differs from alpine skiing in that you ski on the flat and go uphill as well as downhill. Special skis are used.

Nordic combined. A cross-country skiing competition which includes both ski jumping and individual racing.

Off-piste. Unpisted runs - natural rather than beaten snow.

Outside ski. The term used for the ski outside the curve made when you turn. Outside hip and pole are defined in the same way.

Parallel turn. A turn made with both skis parallel.

Piste. Specially prepared, graded and patrolled alpine runs which are beaten into a smooth surface by machines.

Piste map. A map giving the layout of the runs and lift systems in a resort.

Pole planting. In most turns the inside pole is planted for balance and support as you transfer your weight from one ski to the other.

Powder. Fine, light, dry new snow.

Pre-jumping. Short low jump done to clear a slope edge and avoid being thrown into the air.

Safety strap. Strap attached to the back of some bindings, which ties up around the leg so that the ski is not lost if the binding releases.

Salopettes. Water-resistant skiing dungarees. The advantage of salopettes is that they cover the trunk of your body and keep it warm.

Schussing. Skiing straight down the fall line with the skis parallel.

Side-cut. The "waisted" shape of a ski.

Side-slip. A controlled sideways slide down a slope.

Side-step. Climbing sideways uphill by stepping up one ski at a time and edging it into the slope.

Skating. A method of increasing speed by stepping one ski at an angle and pushing off from it. You can skate with one or both skis.

Ski Evolotiv. A French method of teaching skiing. Beginners start on very short skis and move on to longer and longer skis as they progress, finishing with full-length skis.

Ski flying. Ski jumping done from large hills.

Ski jumping. A nordic event in which skiers jump from specially built hills. They are judged on the style and length of the jump.

Ski stopper. A small, spring loaded brake on a binding. It springs down when the binding is released and digs into the snow to stop the ski from sliding downhill.

Slalom. The term for turning through a series of gates down a course. In alpine competitions there are four slalom events: slalom, giant slalom, supergiant slalom and parallel slalom.

Snow-blindness. Blindness caused by strong glare at high altitudes when no glasses or goggles are worn. It may be temporary but can also result in permanent eye damage.

Snowplough. Gliding with the skis opened in a "V" shape, tips together and tails apart and most pressure on the inside edges. It is the simplest way of controlling speed.

Snowplough turn. A simple turn made in the snowplough position by putting more pressure on the outside ski.

Stem christie. A turn made from a traverse by pushing out the upper or lower ski into a half snowplough.

Stemming. Skiing with one ski at an angle to the other (half a snowplough).

Stop swing. A method for coming to a halt with your skis parallel by swinging them round at right angles to the fall line.

Soup. Wet, heavy snow found in warm conditions.

Telemark. A cross-country turn invented by Sondre Norheim and named after his home town in Norway. The outside ski is moved forward until the boot is next to the tip of the inside ski. The skier sinks down, bending the inside knee low as the ouside ski steers the turn.

Tracks. Parallel ski-width tracks made by machines for cross-country skiing.

Traversing. Skiing across the fall line.

Unweighted ski. A ski which is bearing little or no weight.

Unweighting. Term used for a momentary reduction of weight on the skis prior to a turn. It can be done by quickly straightening the body (up-unweighting) or suddenly bending low (down-unweighting).

Uphill turn. A turn made up the slope (away from the fall line). It is used for braking and stopping.

Upper ski. Term used for the uppermost ski when skiing across the fall line.

Wax. Substance applied to the surface of skis in order to improve their performance.

Index

Acknowledgements

With thanks to Les Diablerets Tourist
Office and to the Y.H.A..